Flowers and Fairies

Fairy Coloring Book Vol. 2

Author: Jenkie Fontanilla
Illustrator: Audrey Serafica

Flowers and Fairies

Fairy Coloring Book Vol. 2

Author: Jenkie Fontanilla
Illustrator: Audrey Serafica

Short Description

Fairies never cease to amaze.
We give you 40 adorable fairy illustrations for your coloring fun.
This coloring book is suitable for all ages.

Coloring is known to be a stress reliever for adults and
a fun activity between parents and children.
These illustrations will bring out your coloring creativity.
Carefully hand-drawn for passionate colorists out there.
Suitable for children to adult.
Can also be used for personal amusement at home,
school or for family bonding activity with your child.

Tips in Coloring

Color Pencils, watercolors, or crayons will
work together with this coloring book.
Using a marker may bleed on the next page.
When using a marker, it is advised to put cardboard or
any thick paper behind as you color.

Here are some of what's inside this book

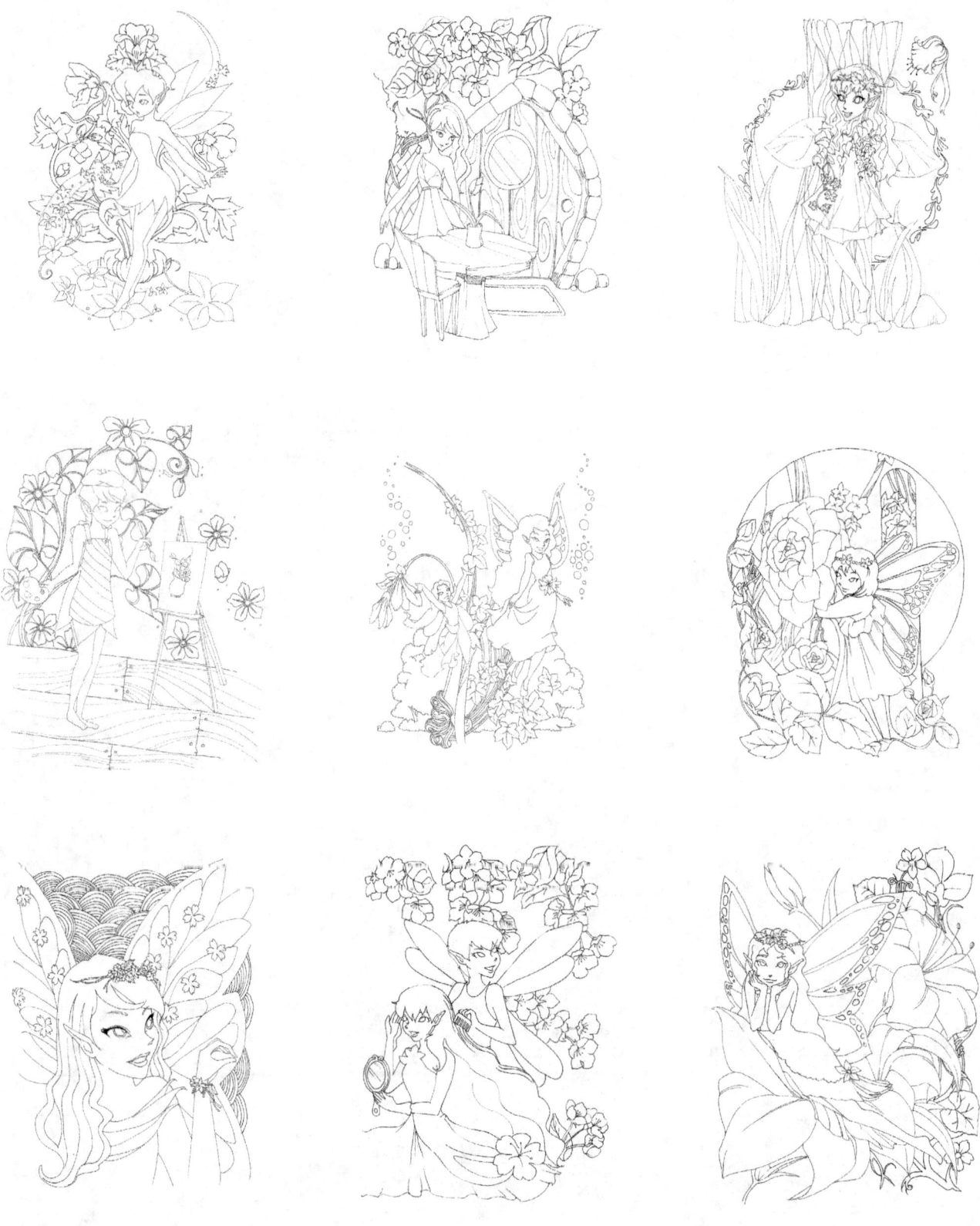

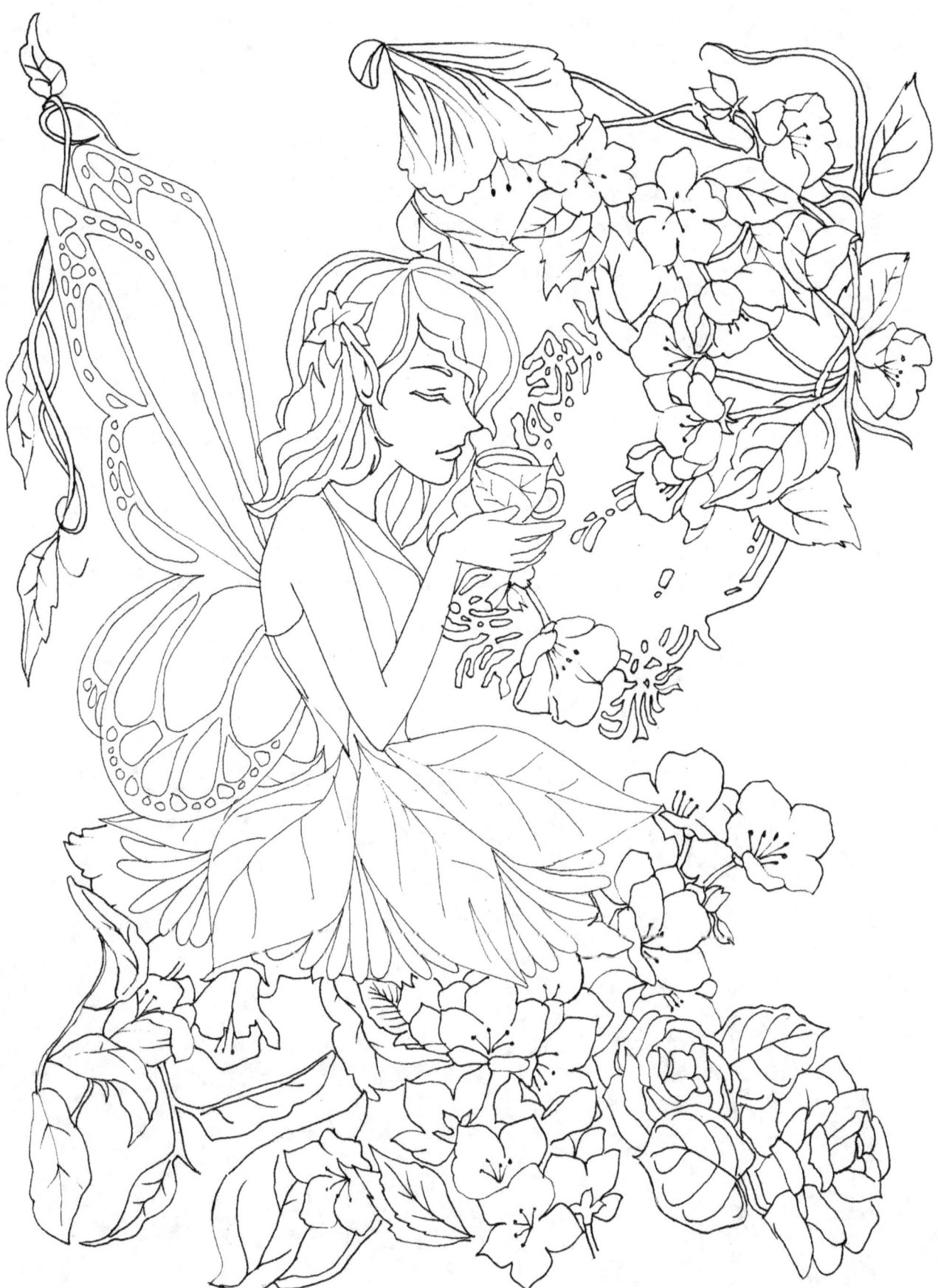

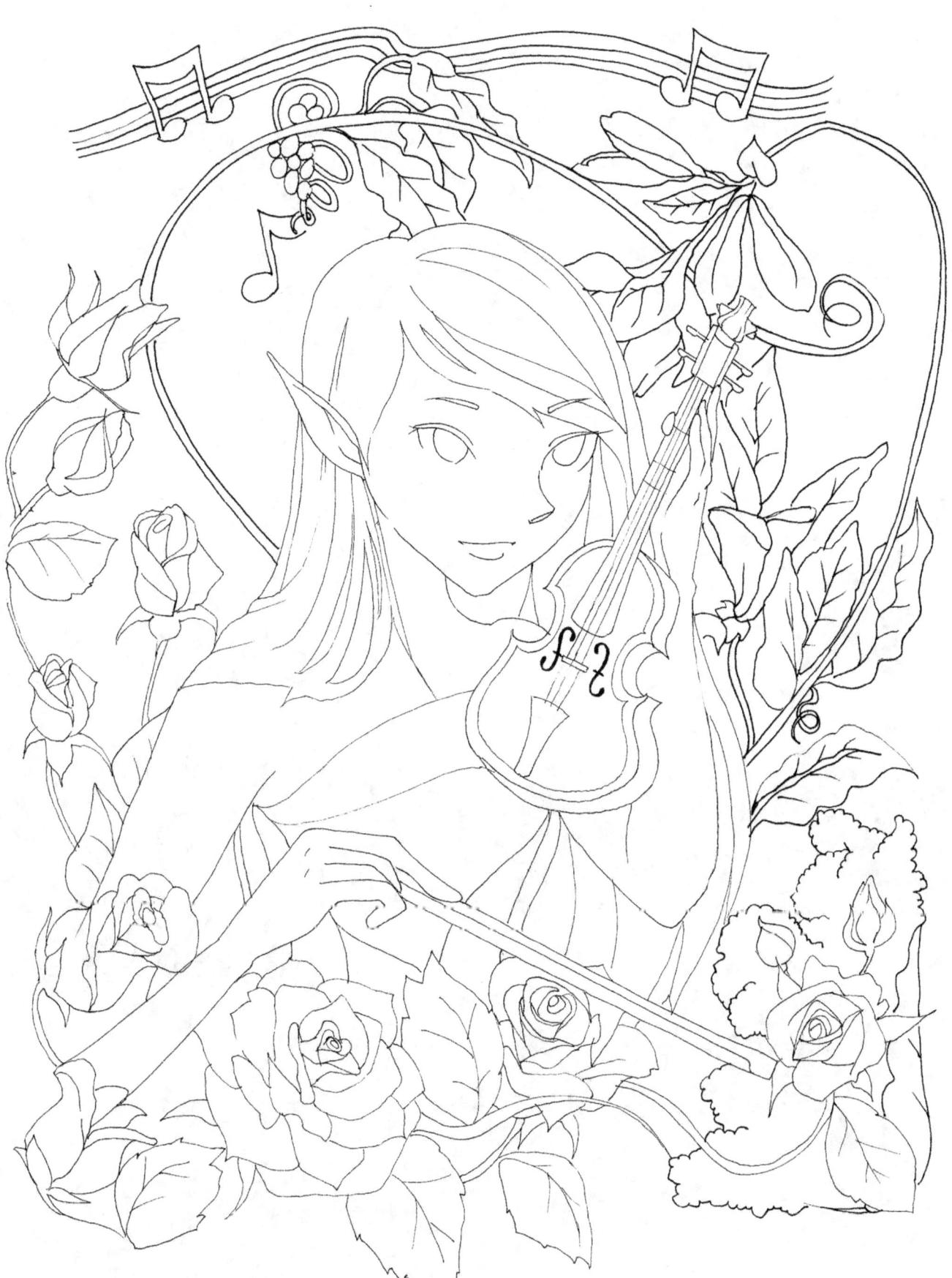

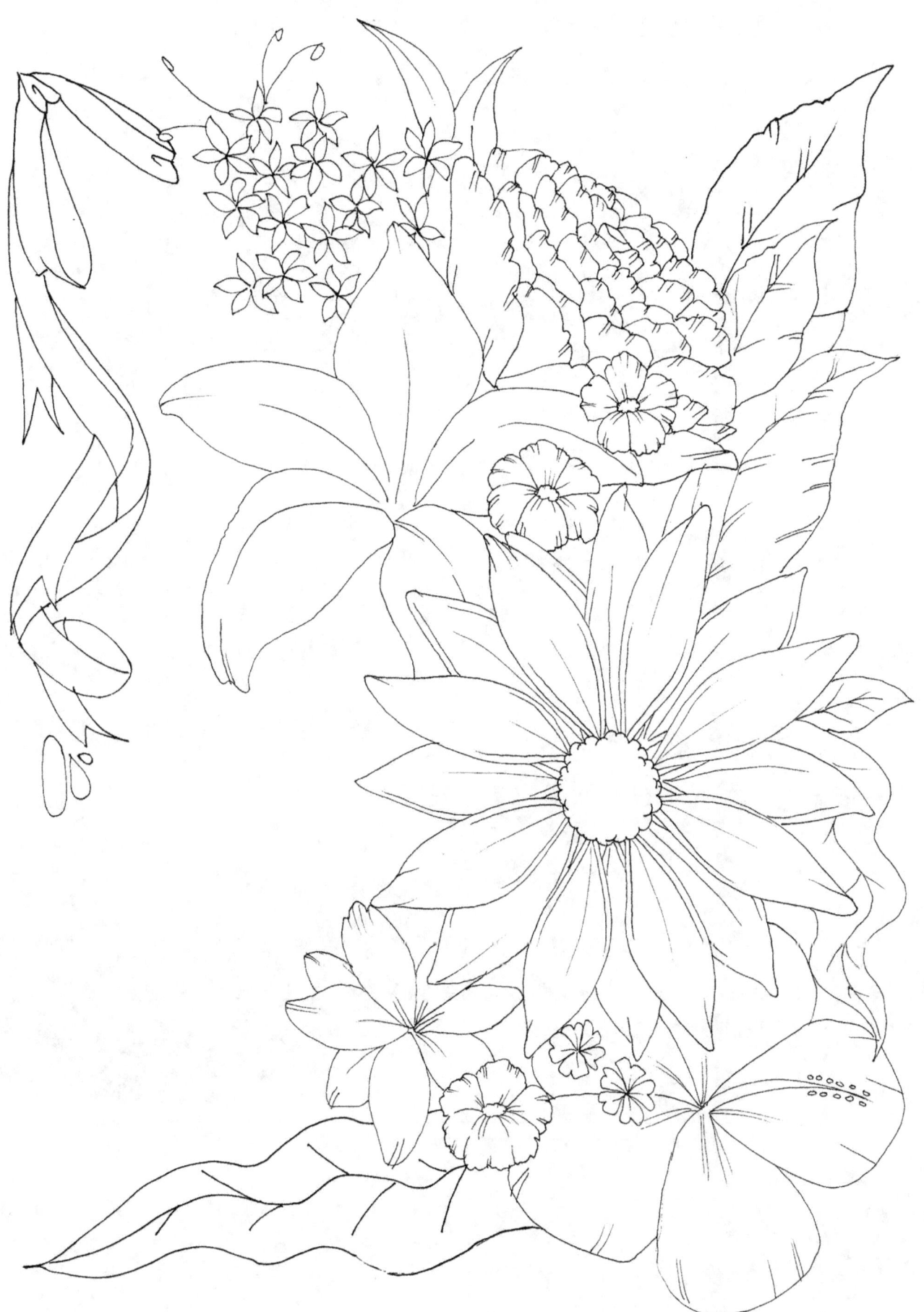

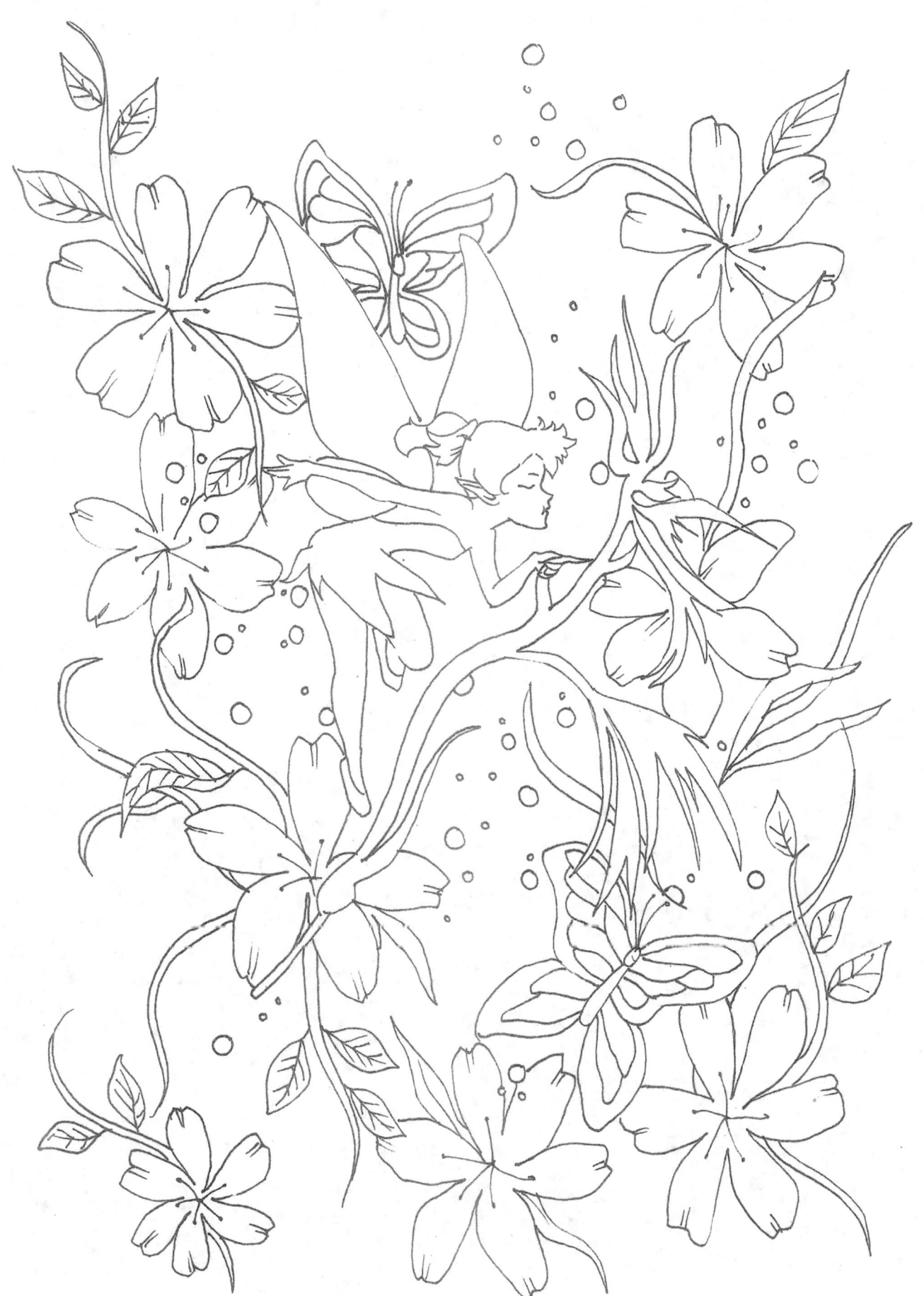

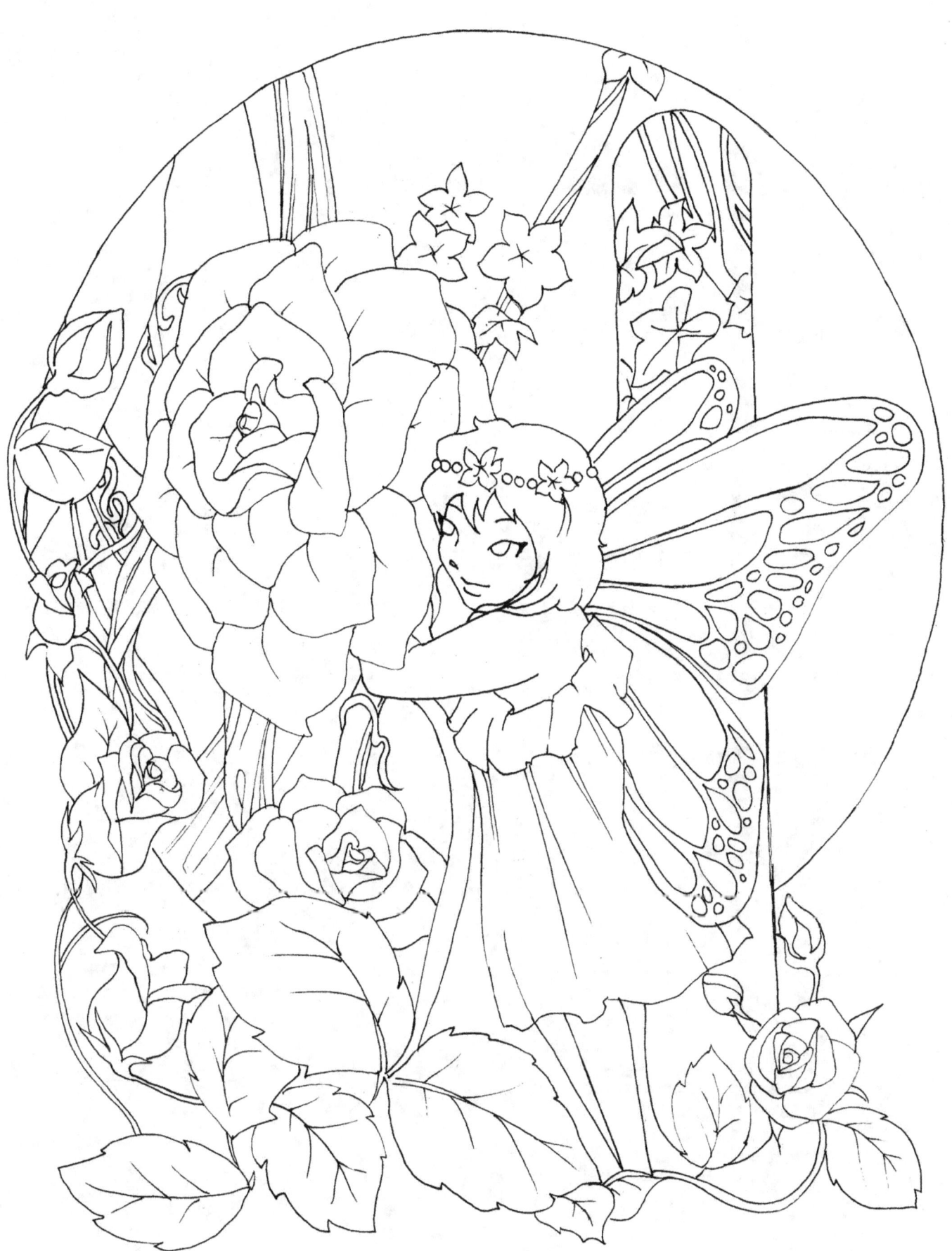

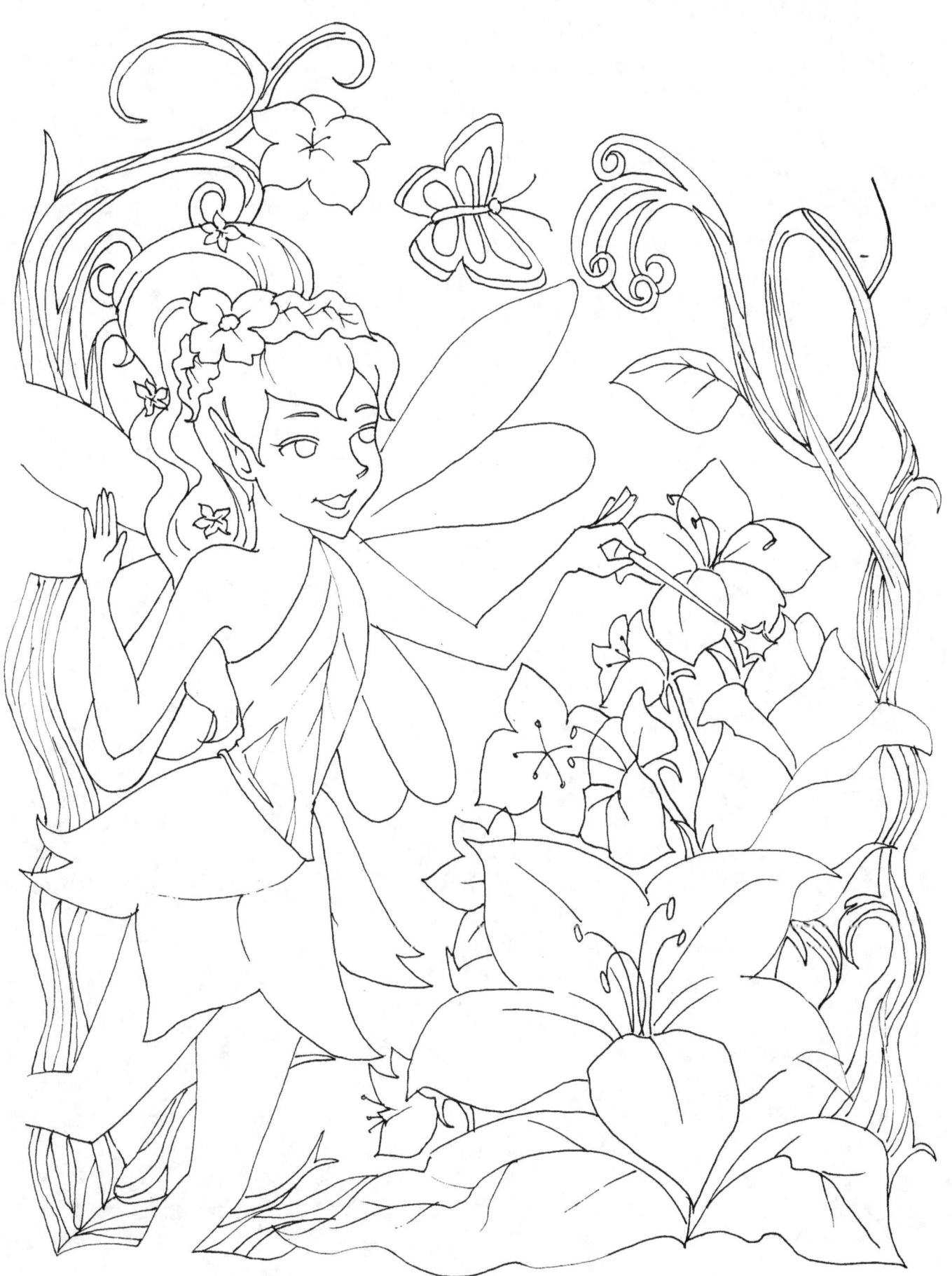

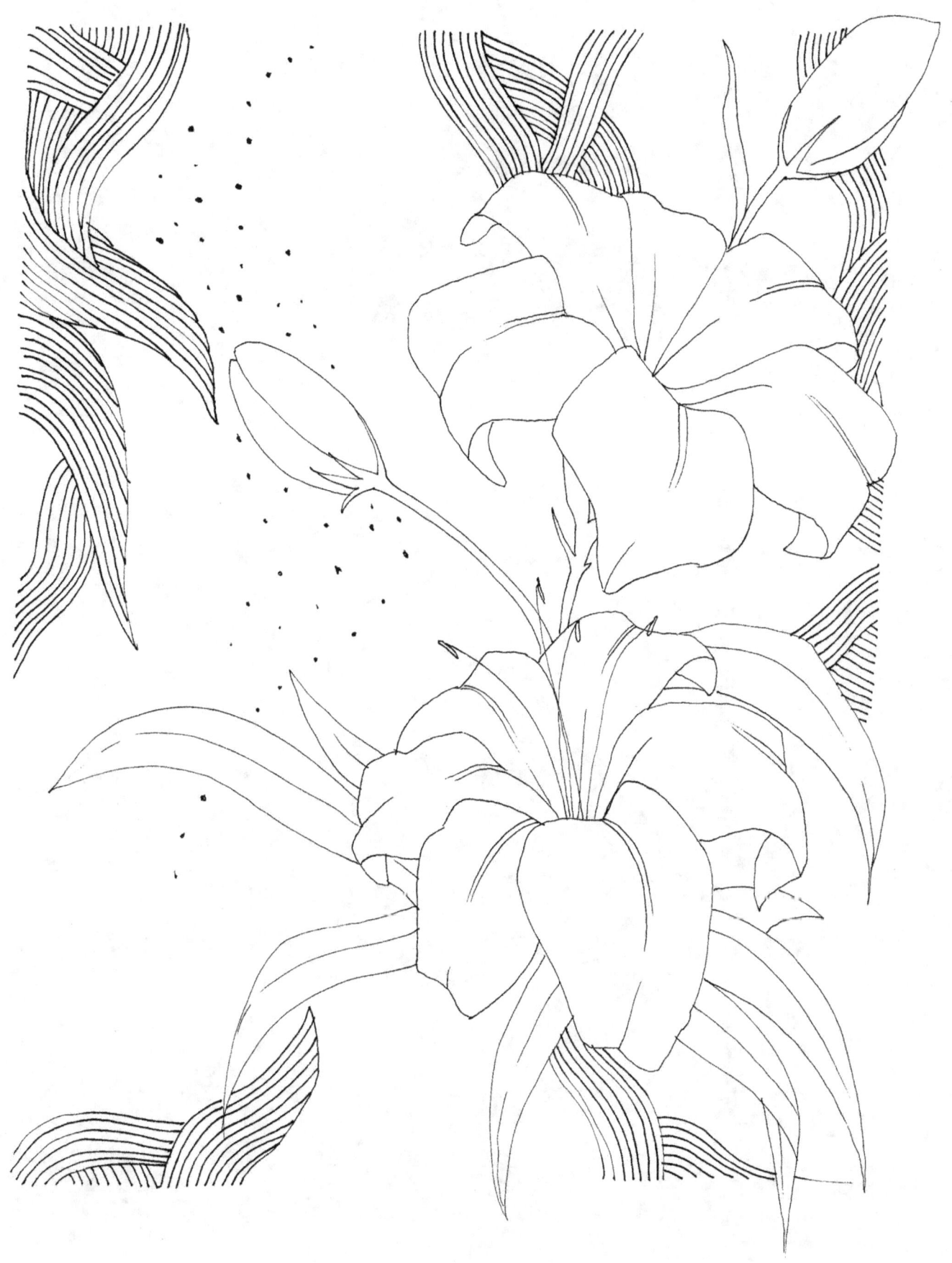

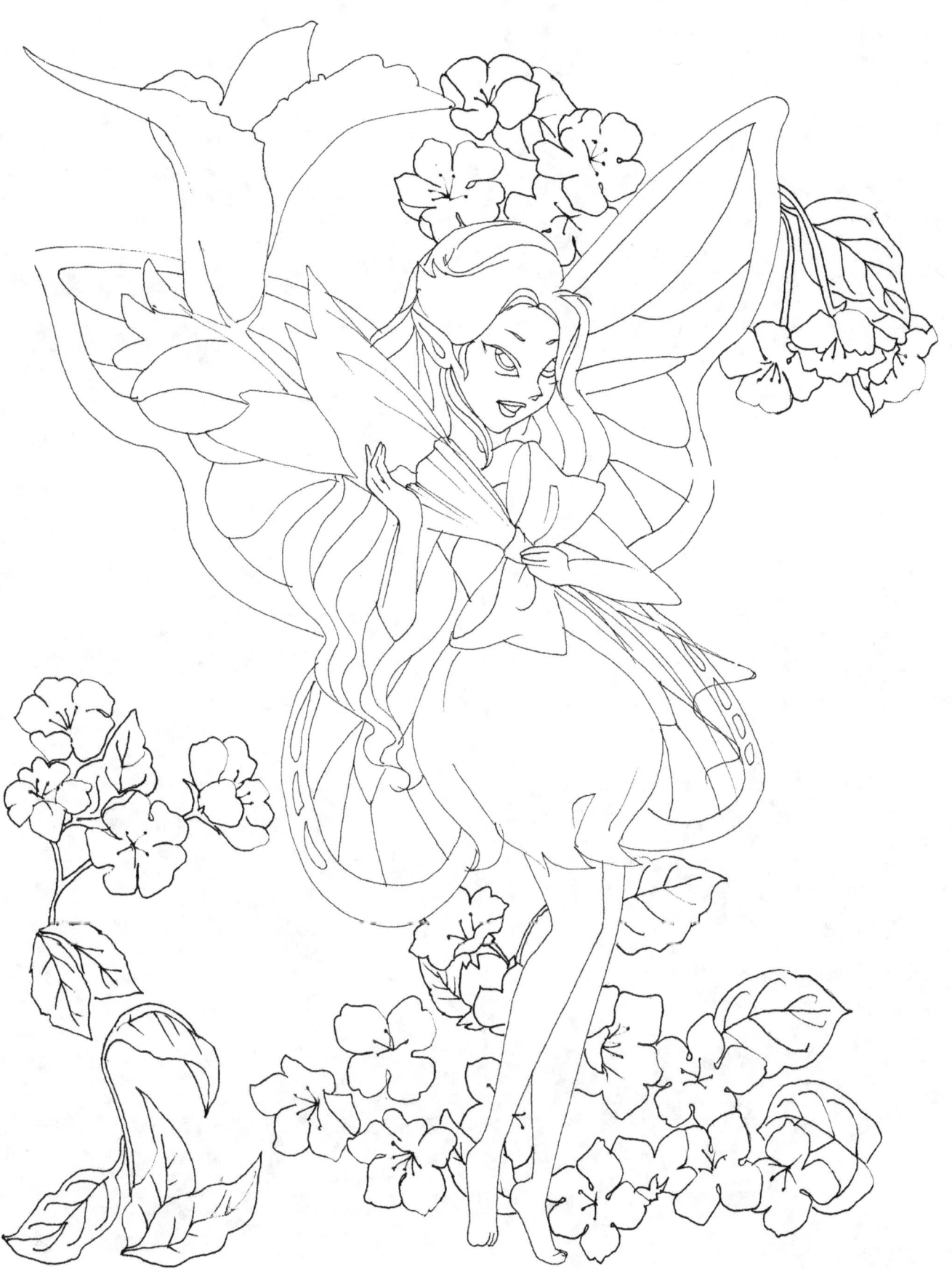

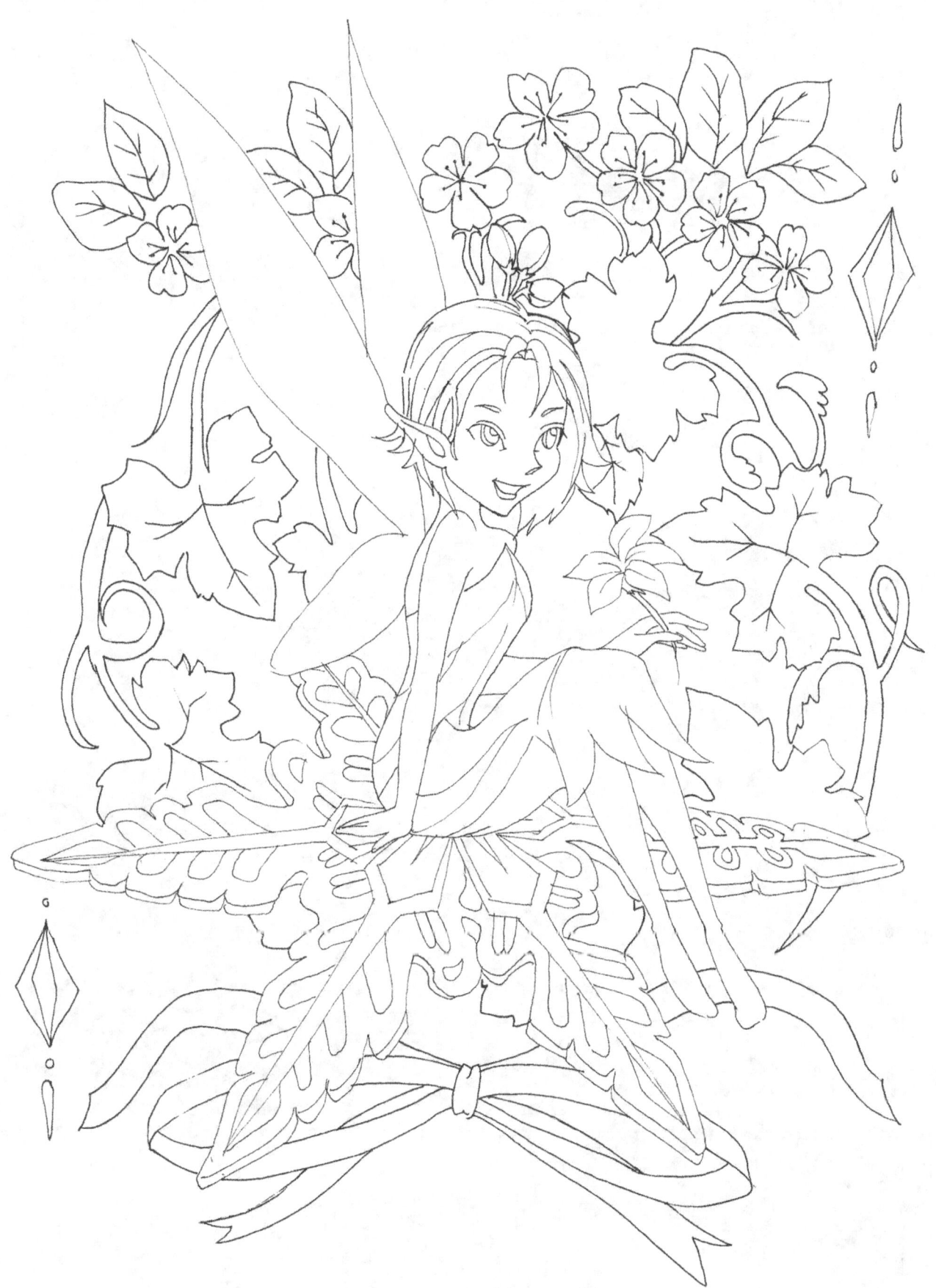

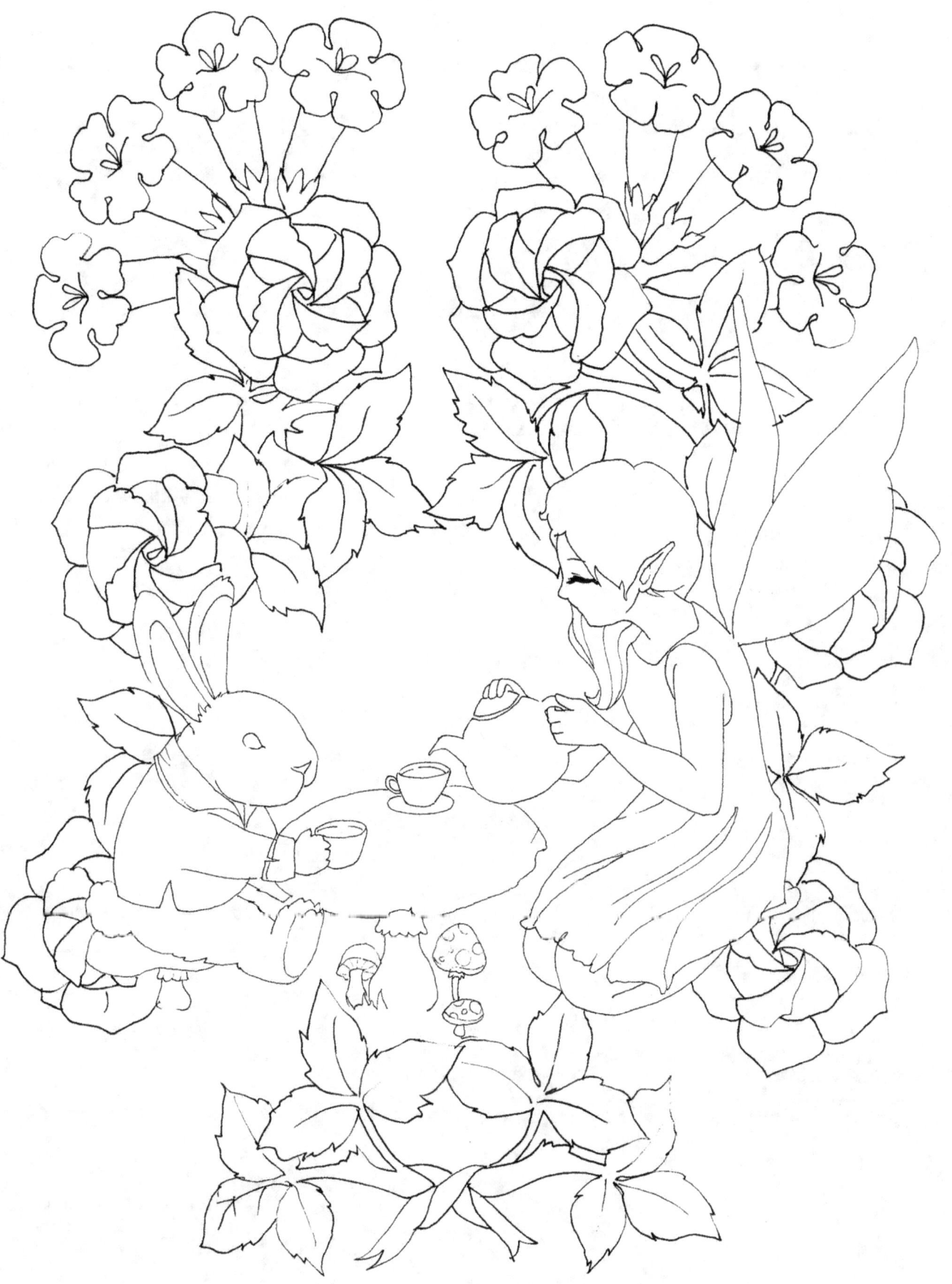

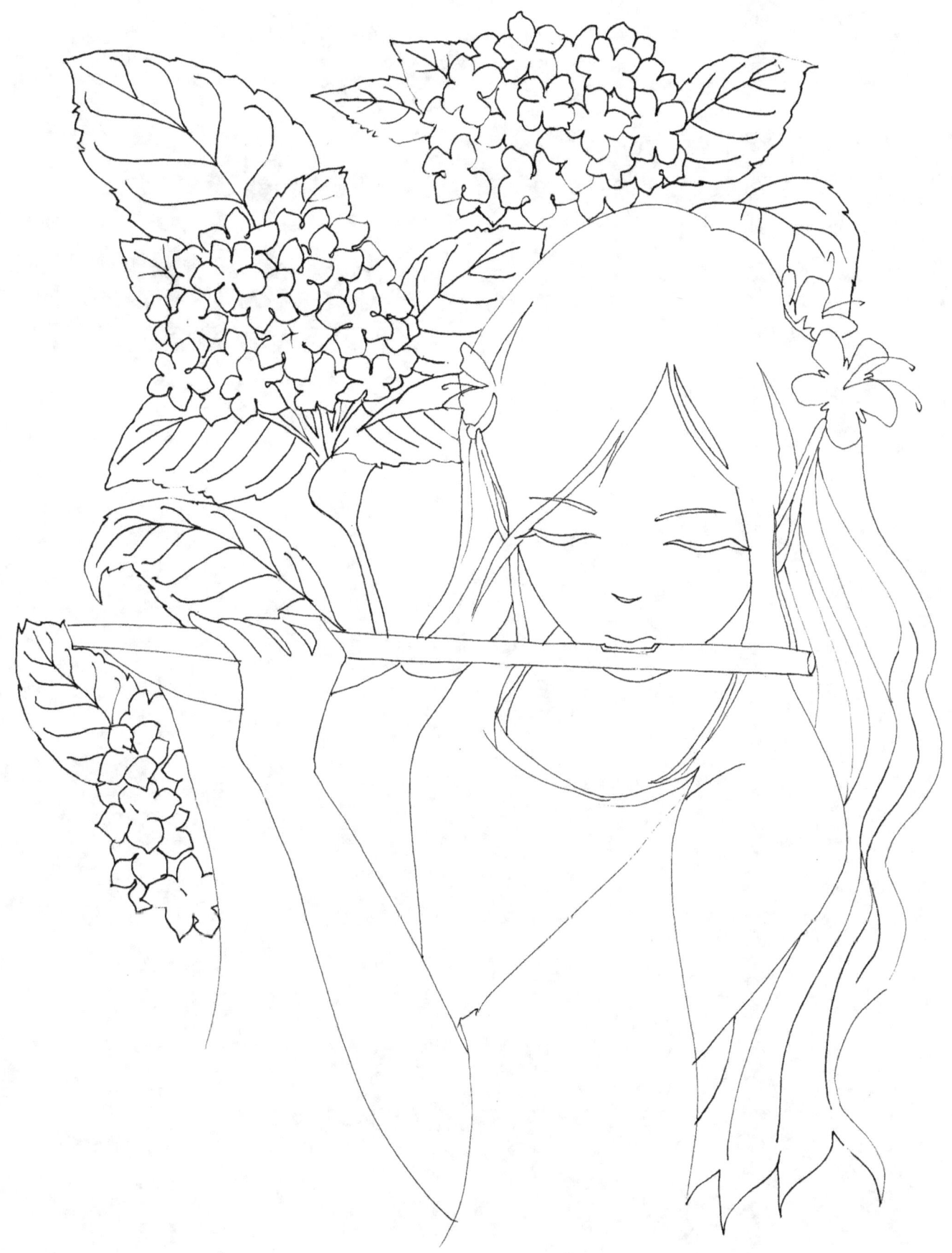

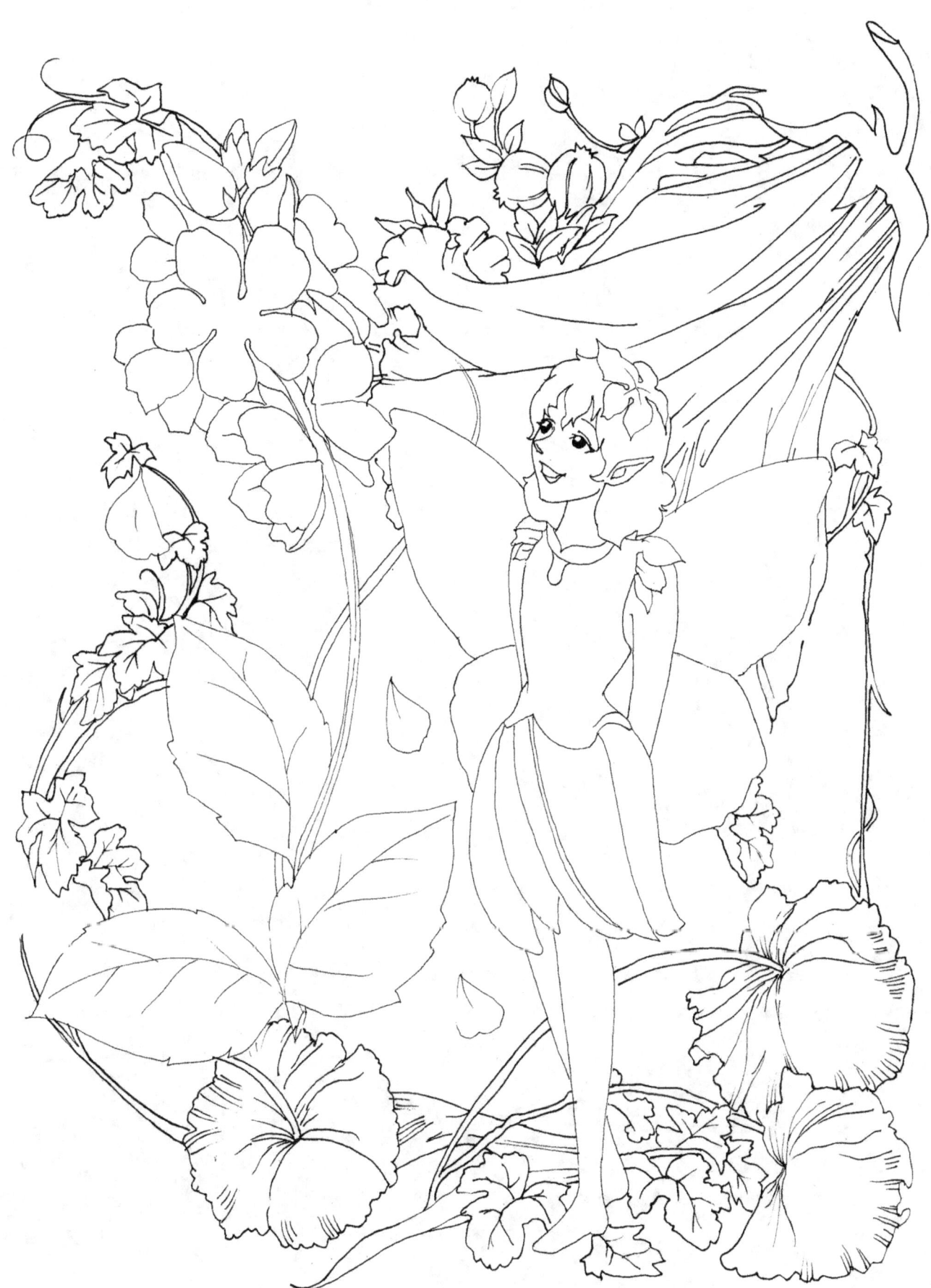

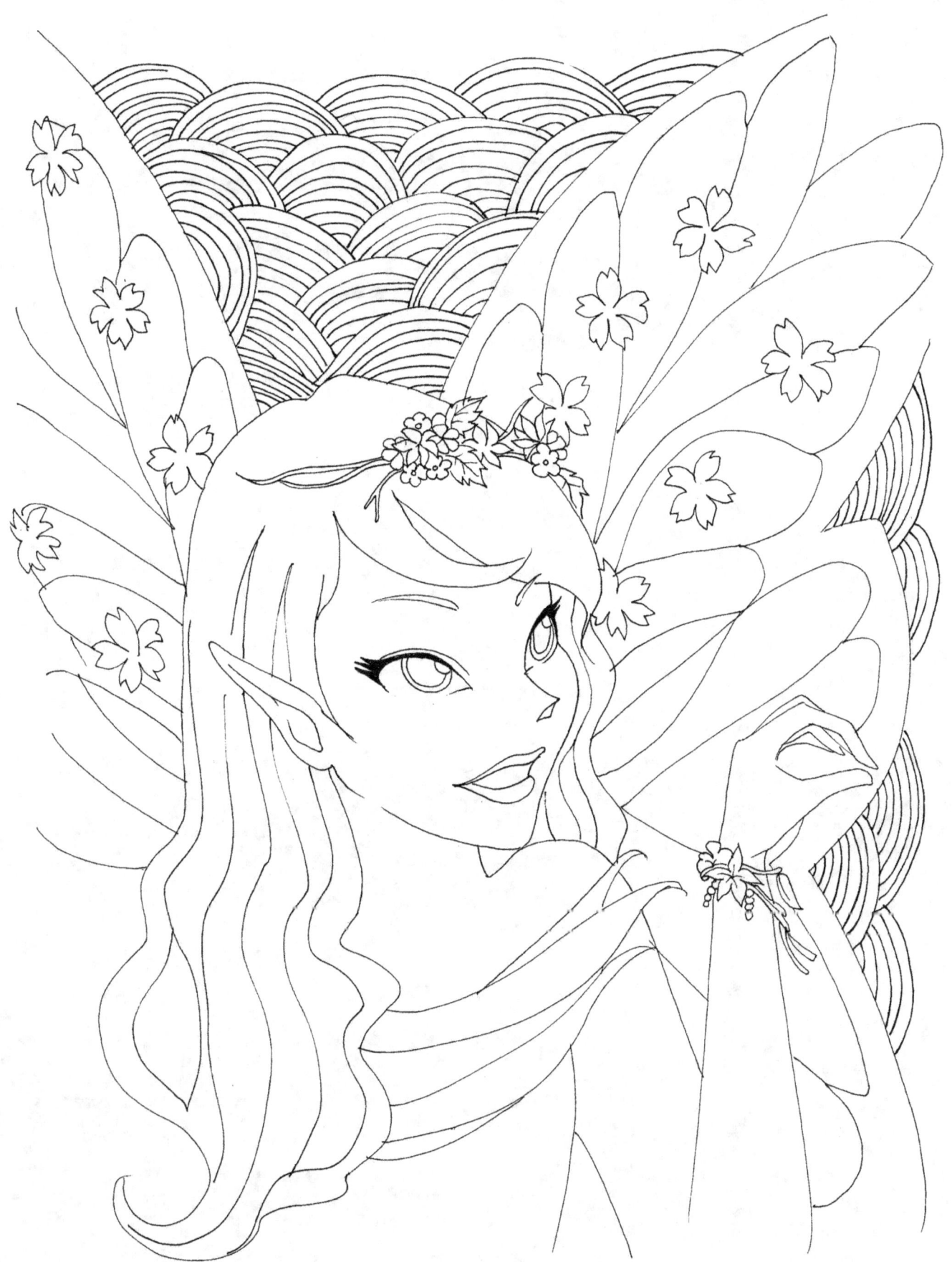

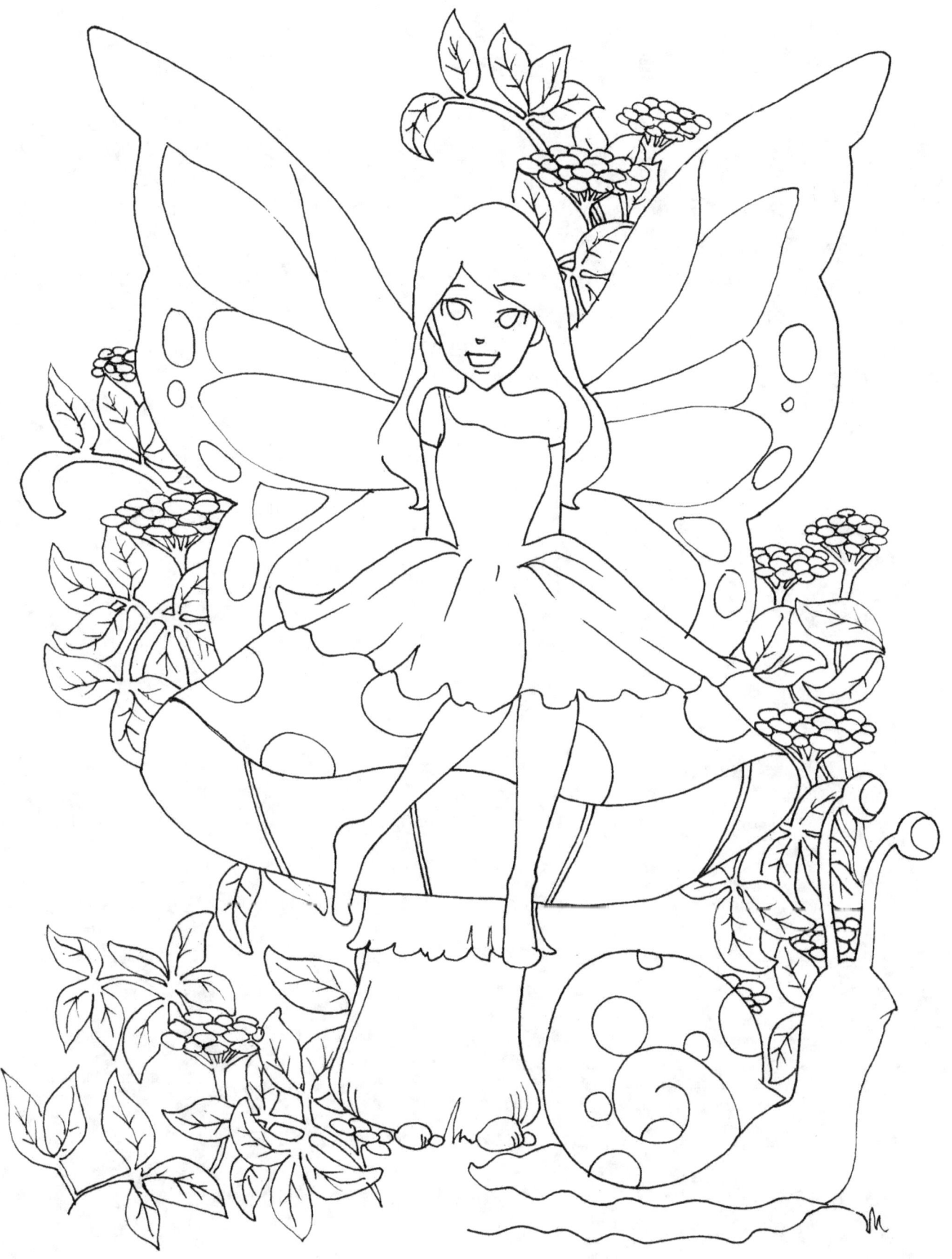

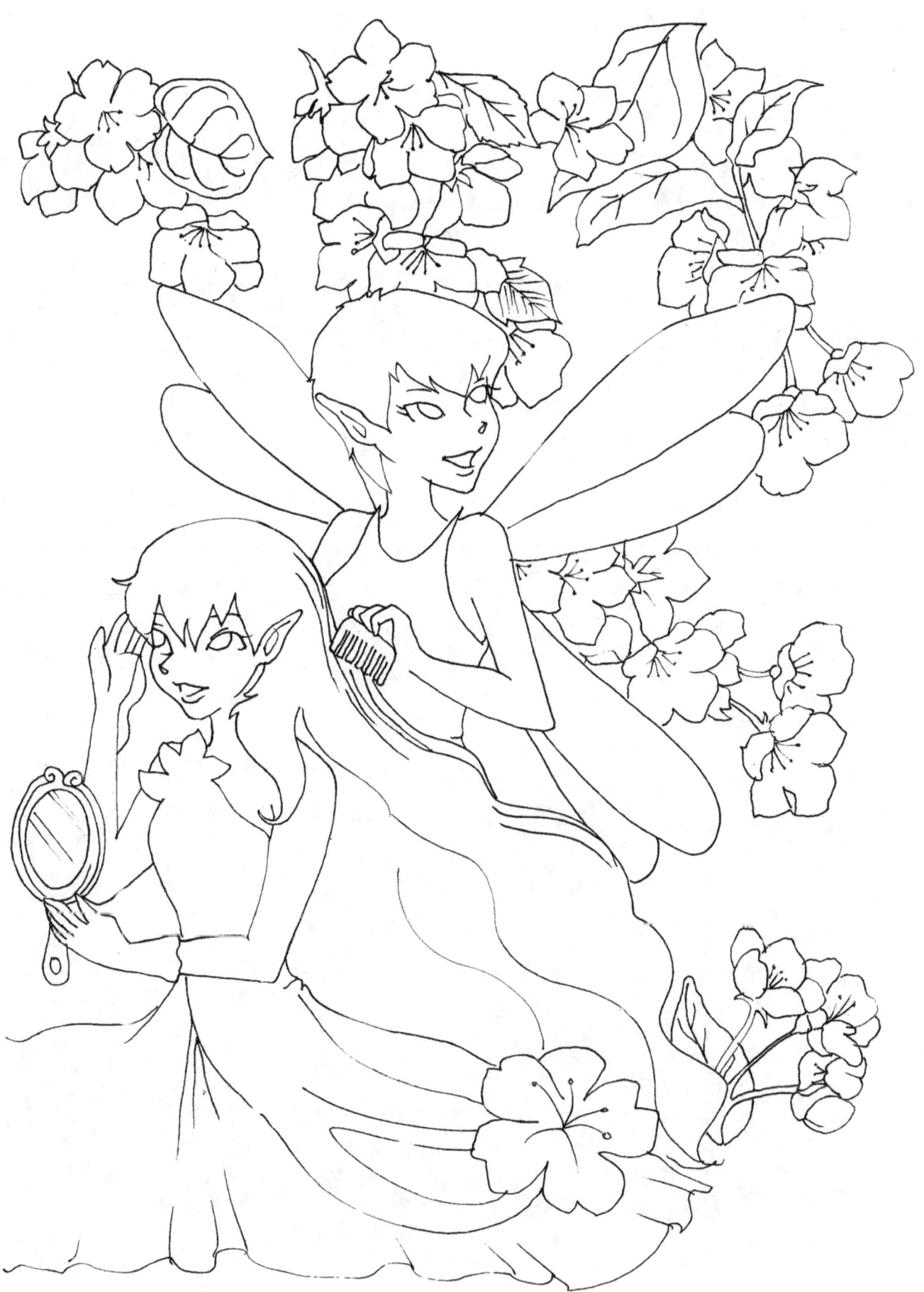

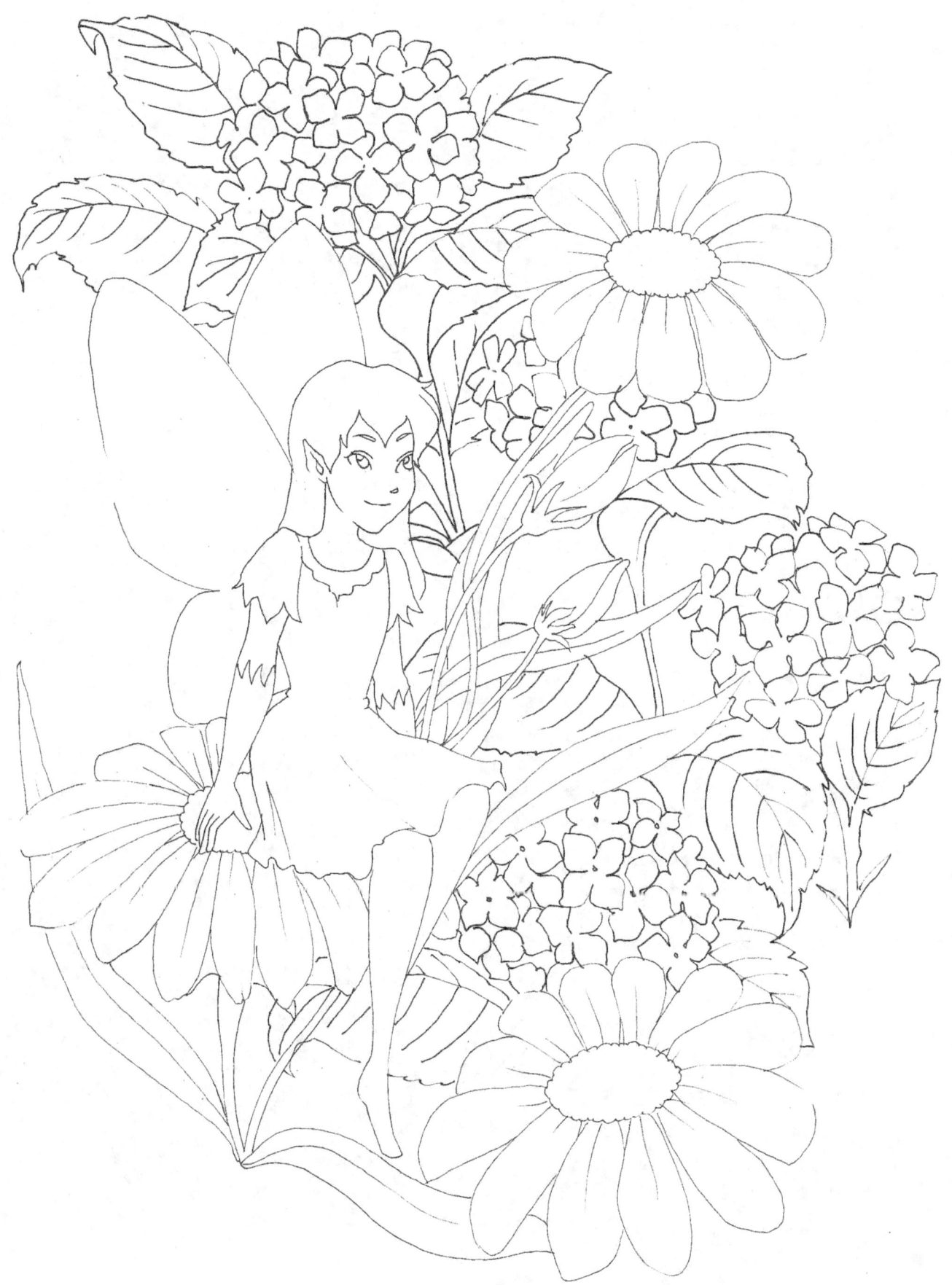

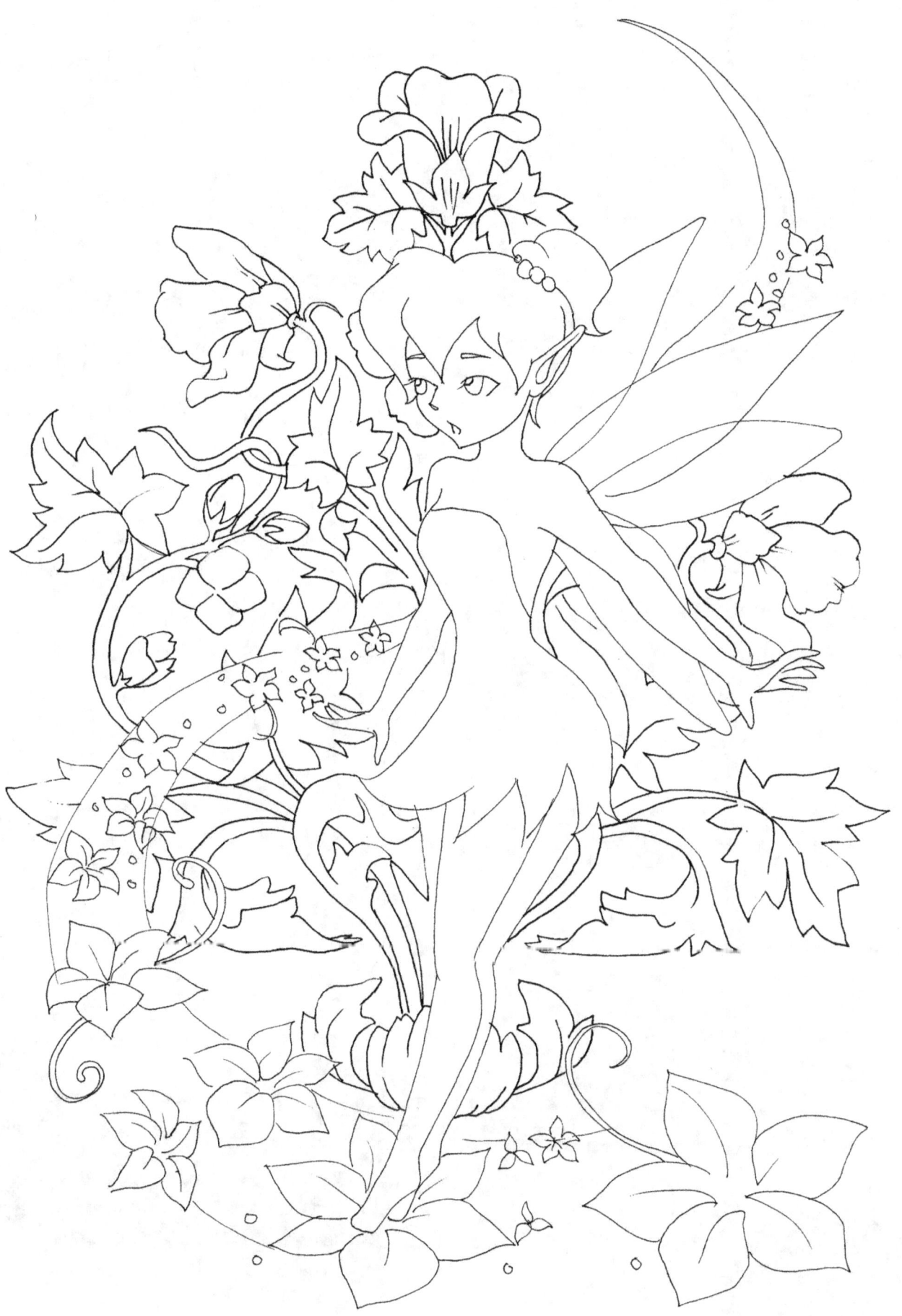

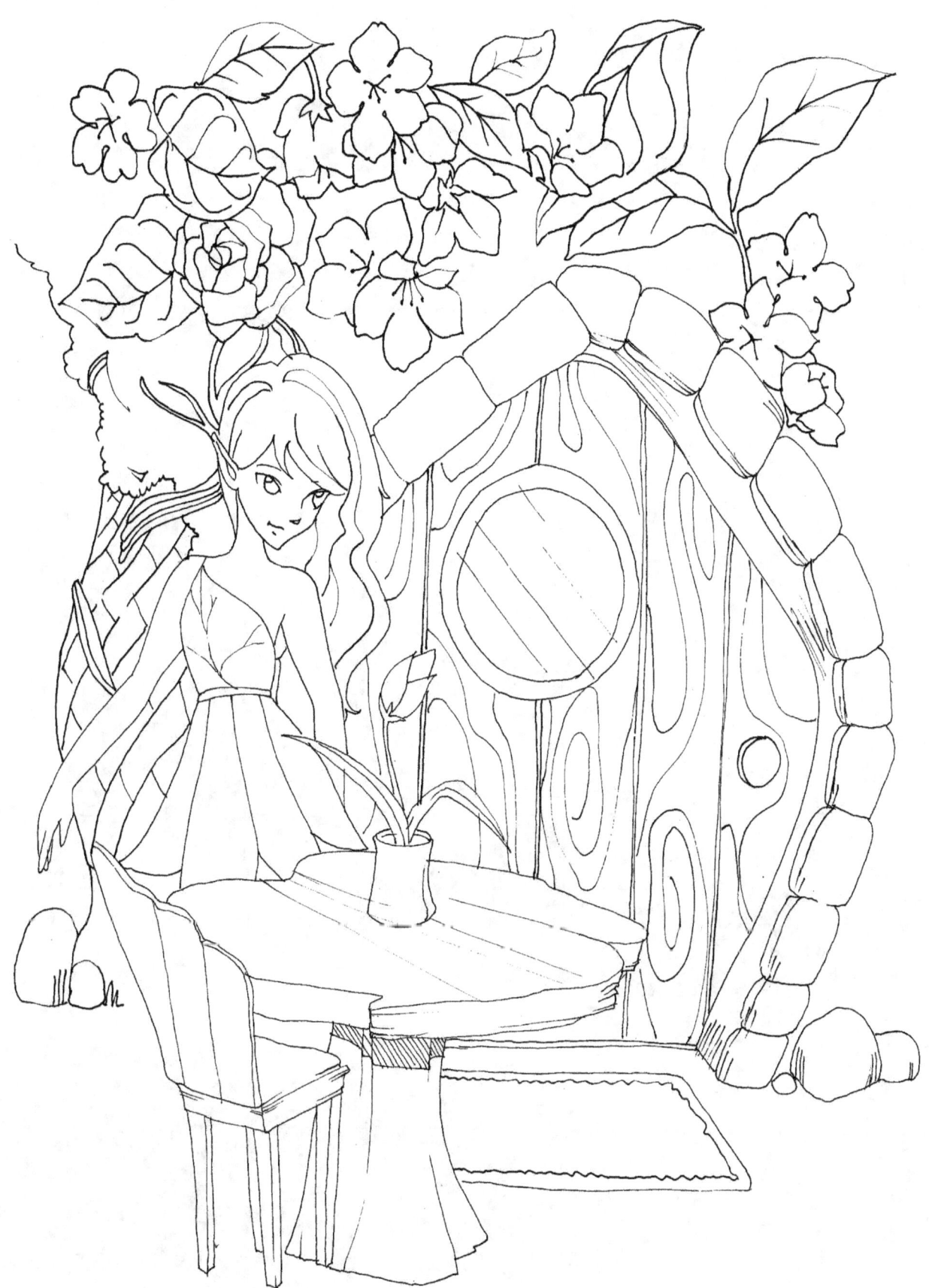

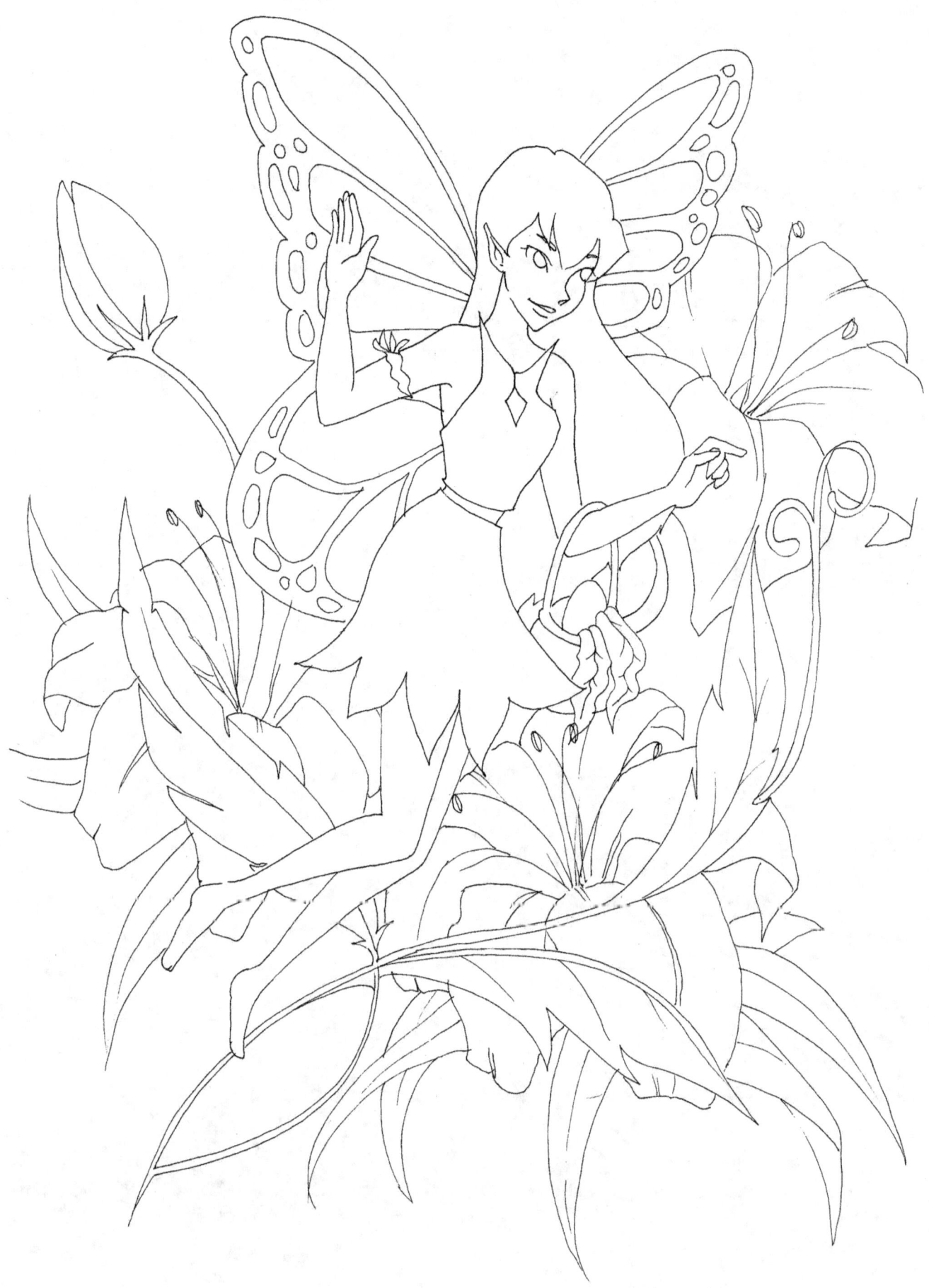

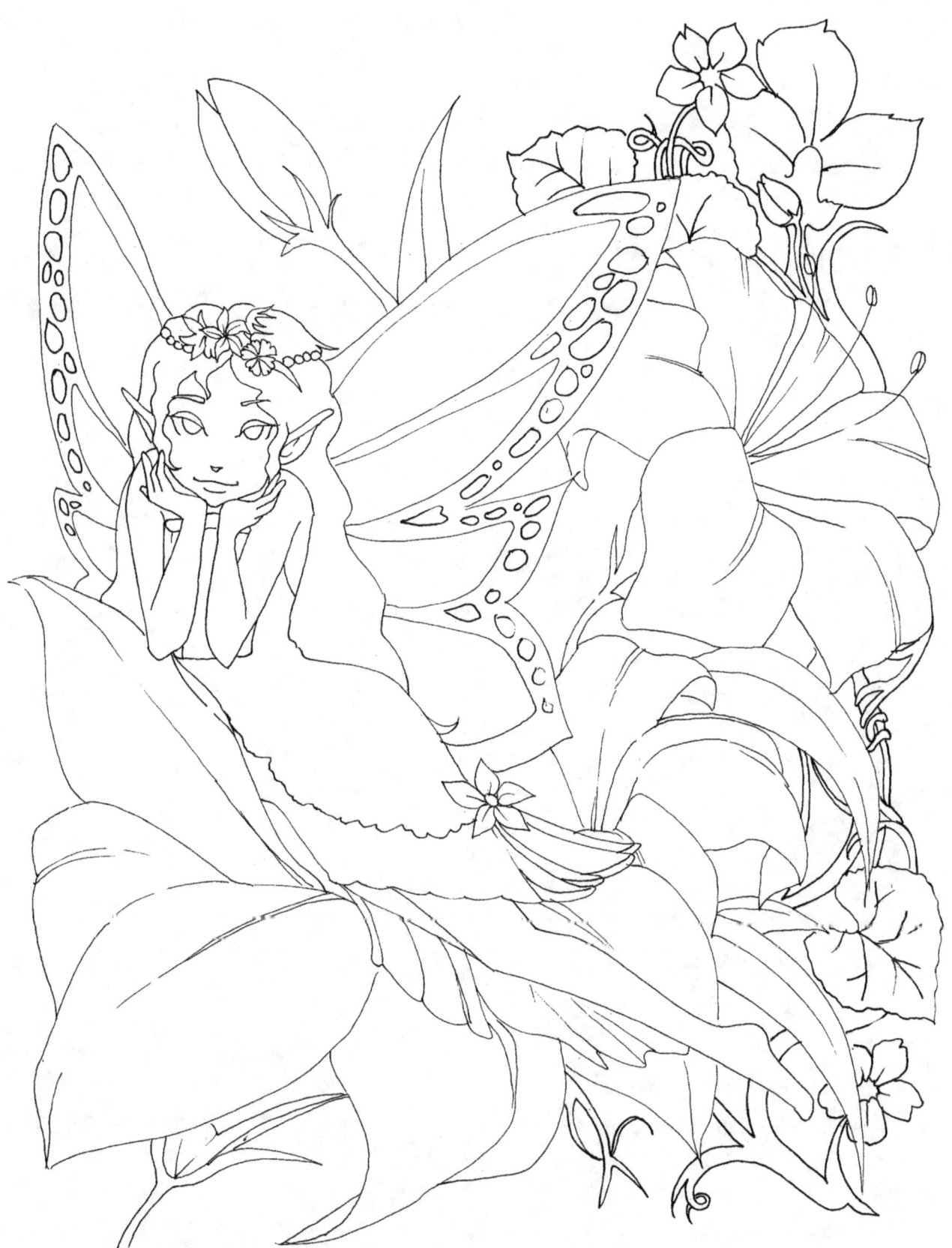

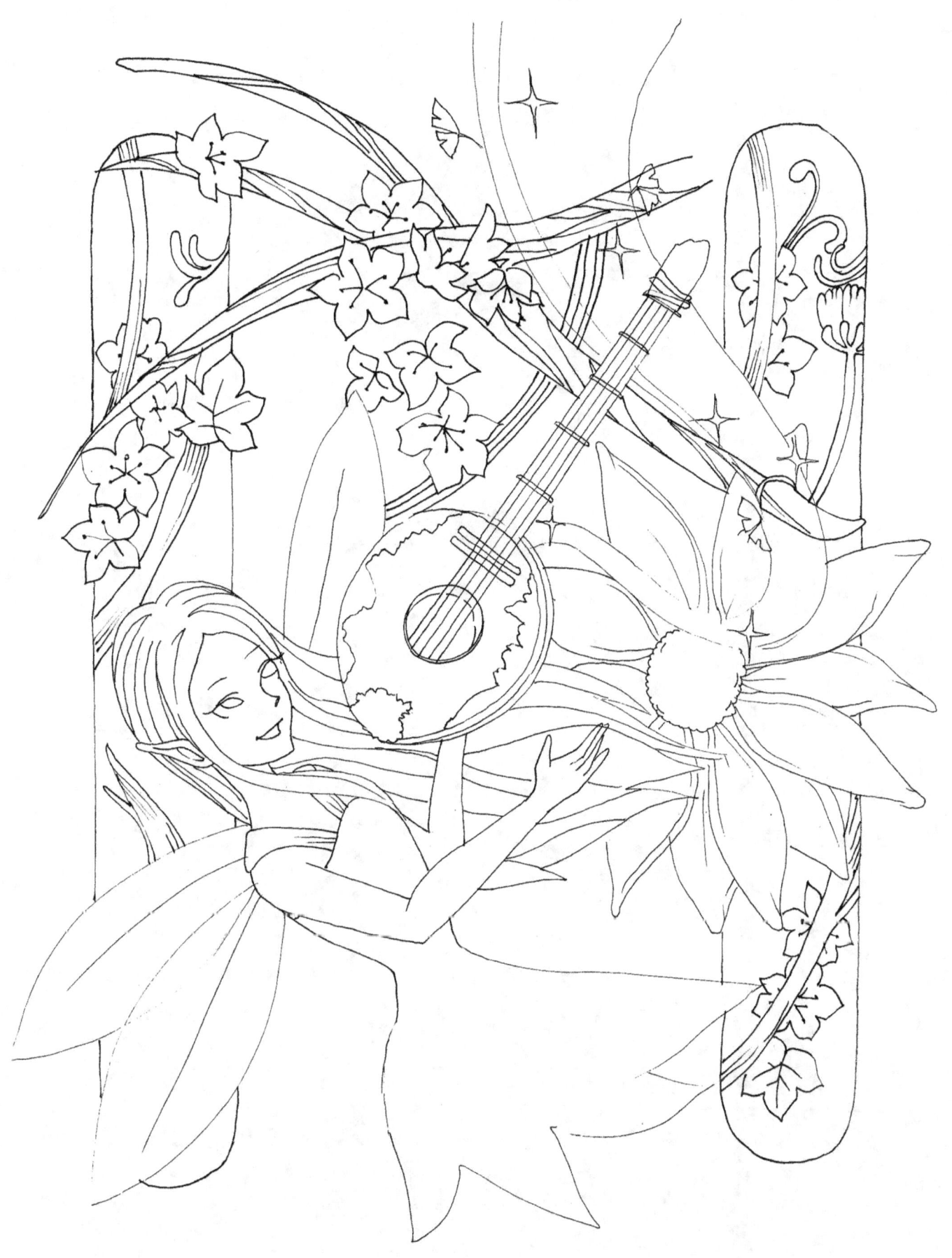

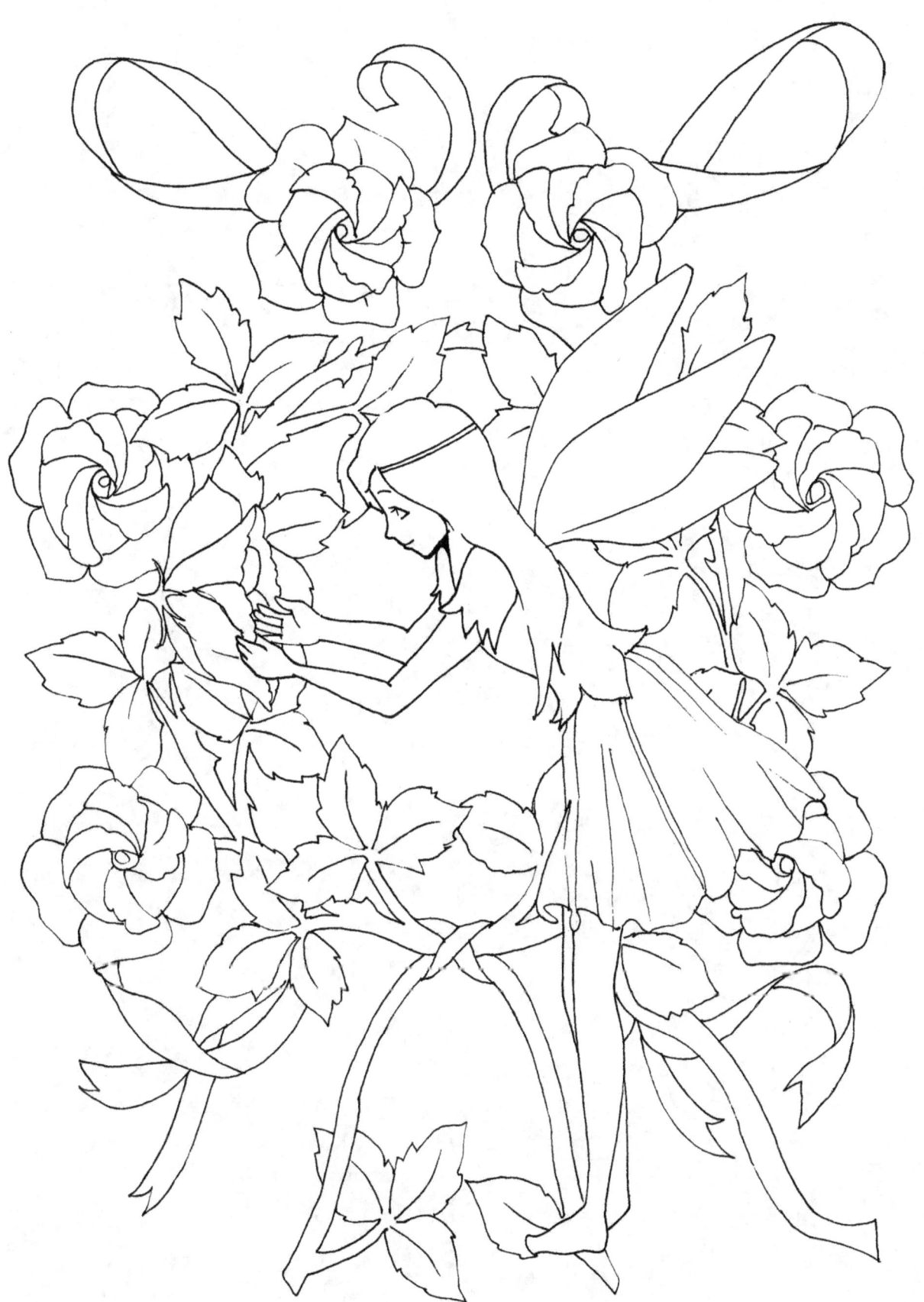

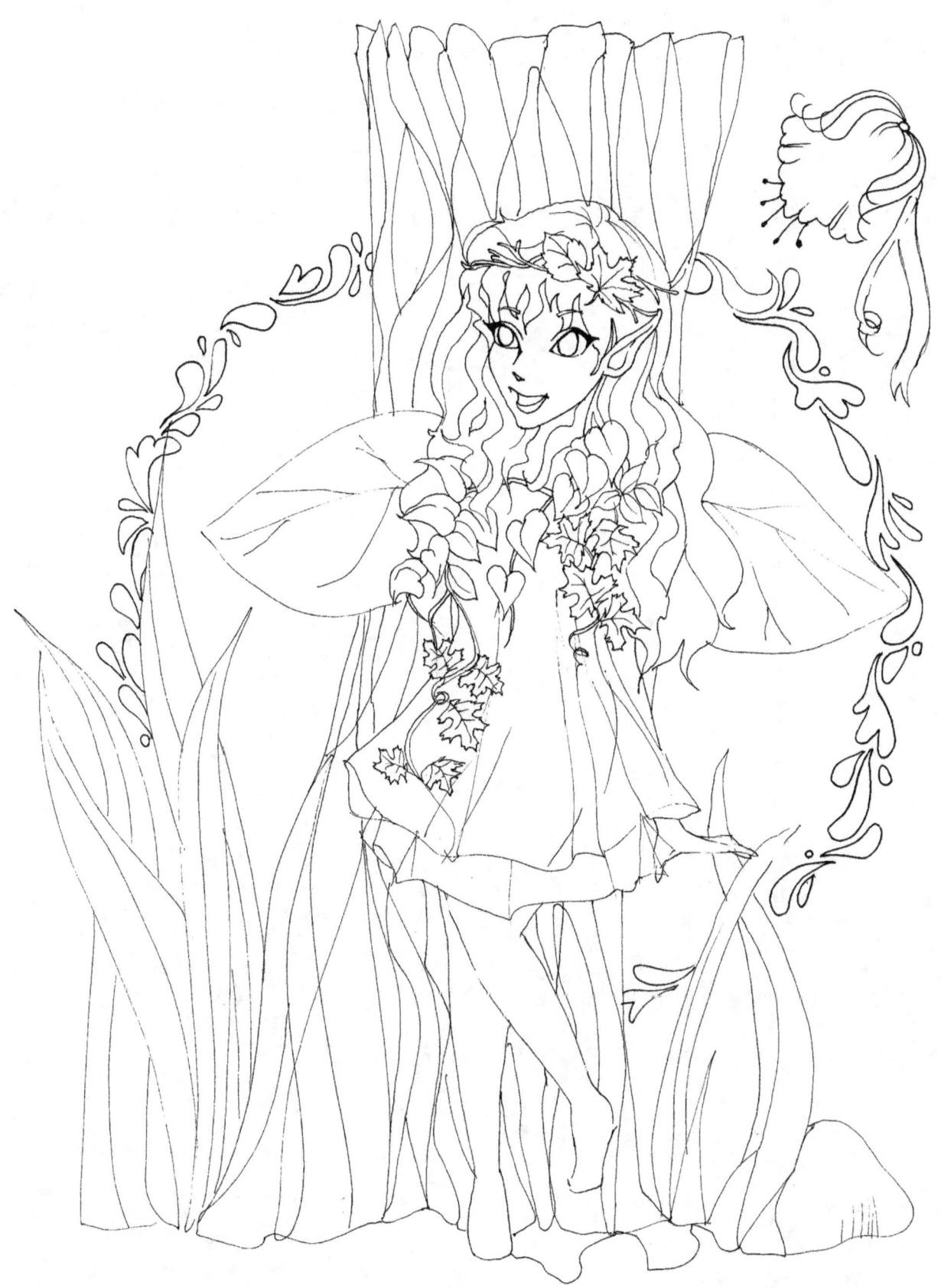

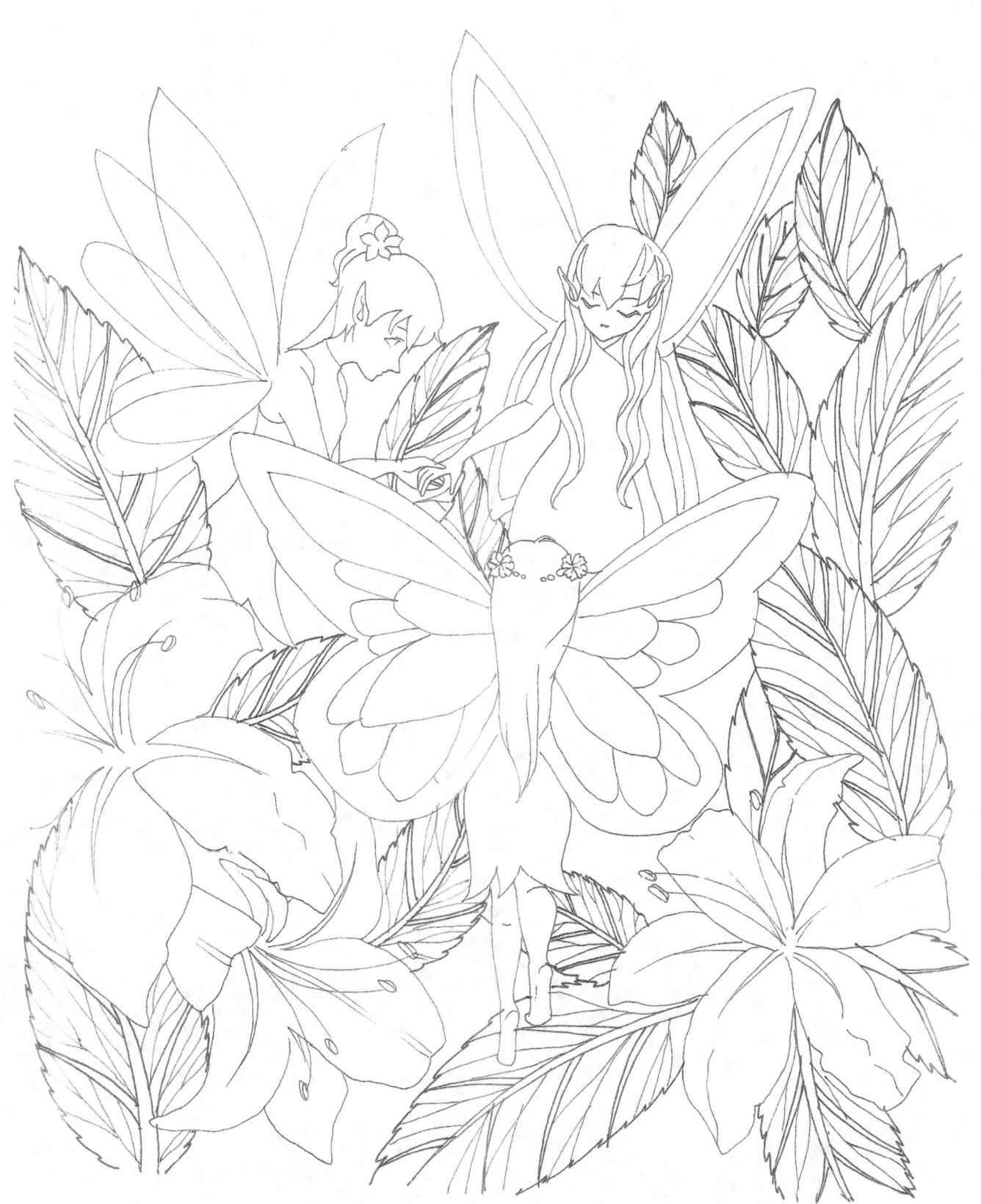

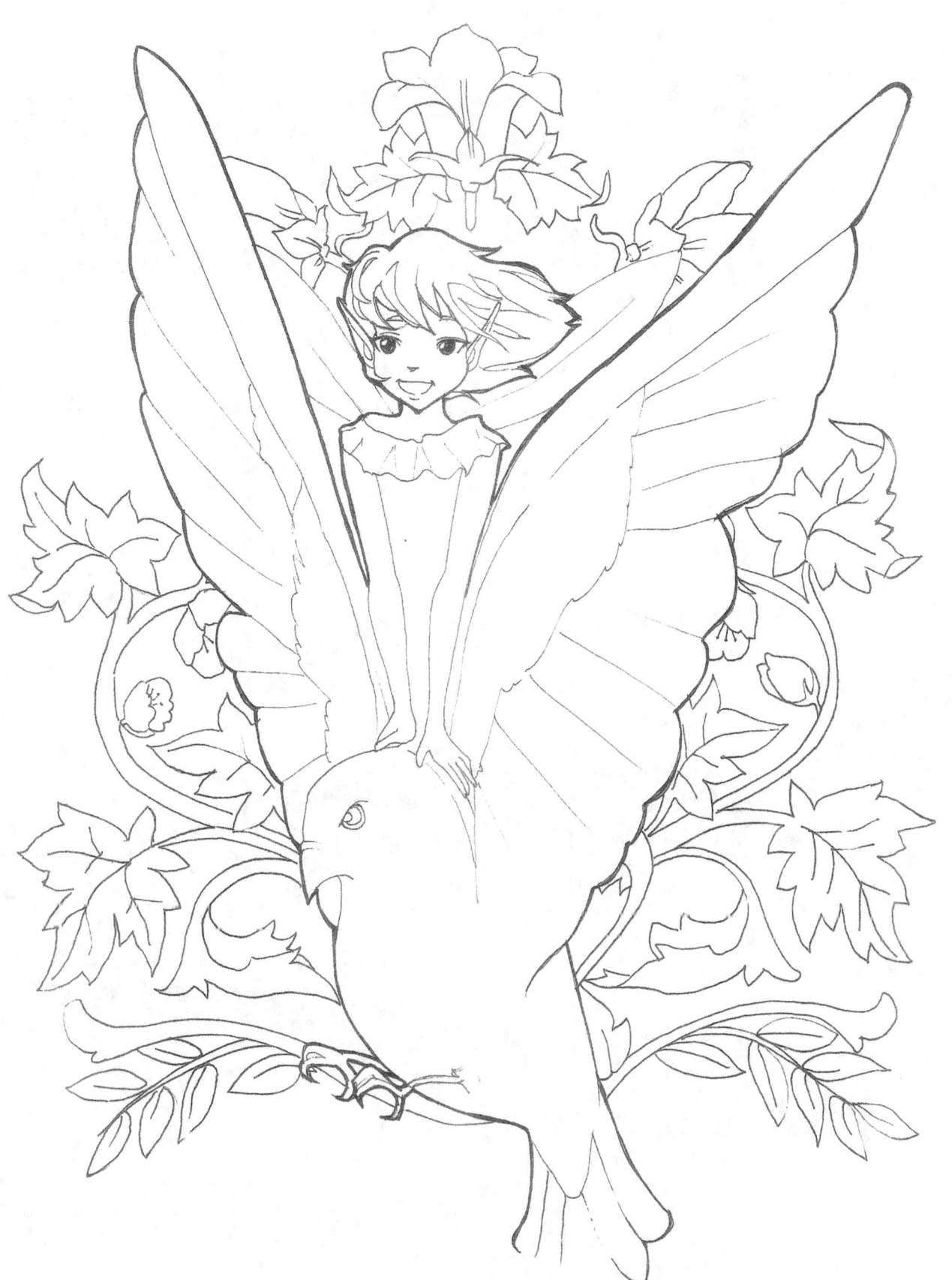

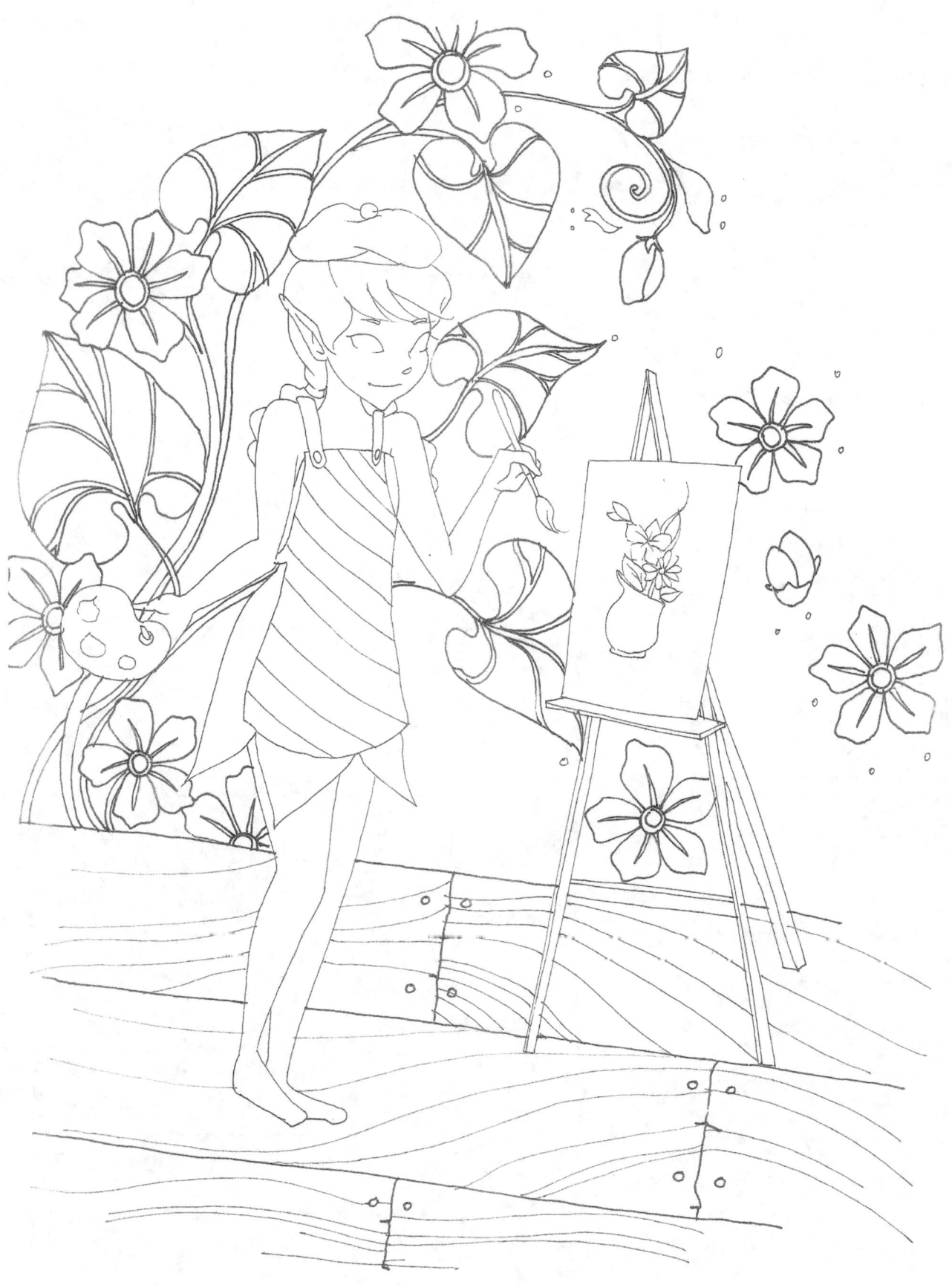

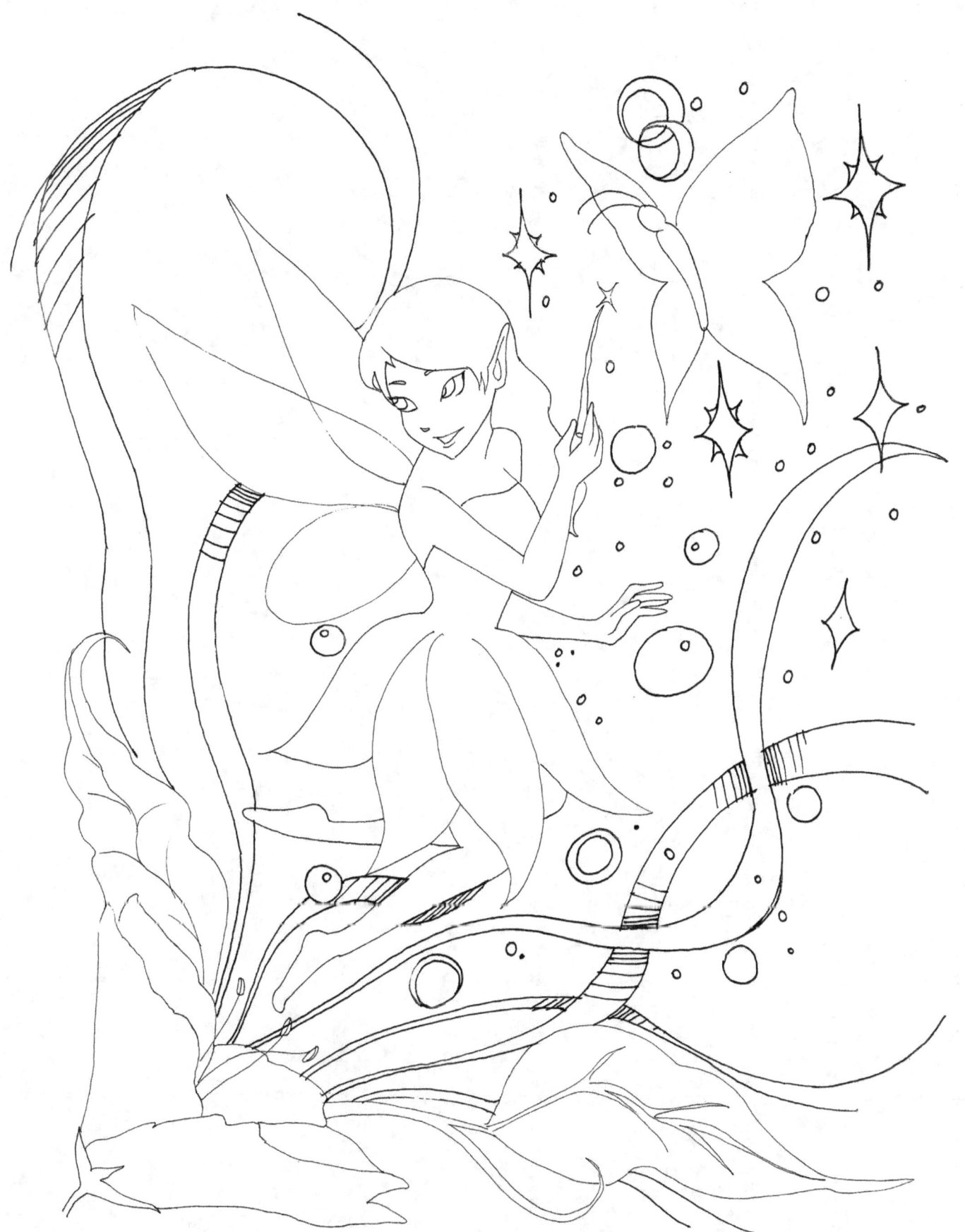

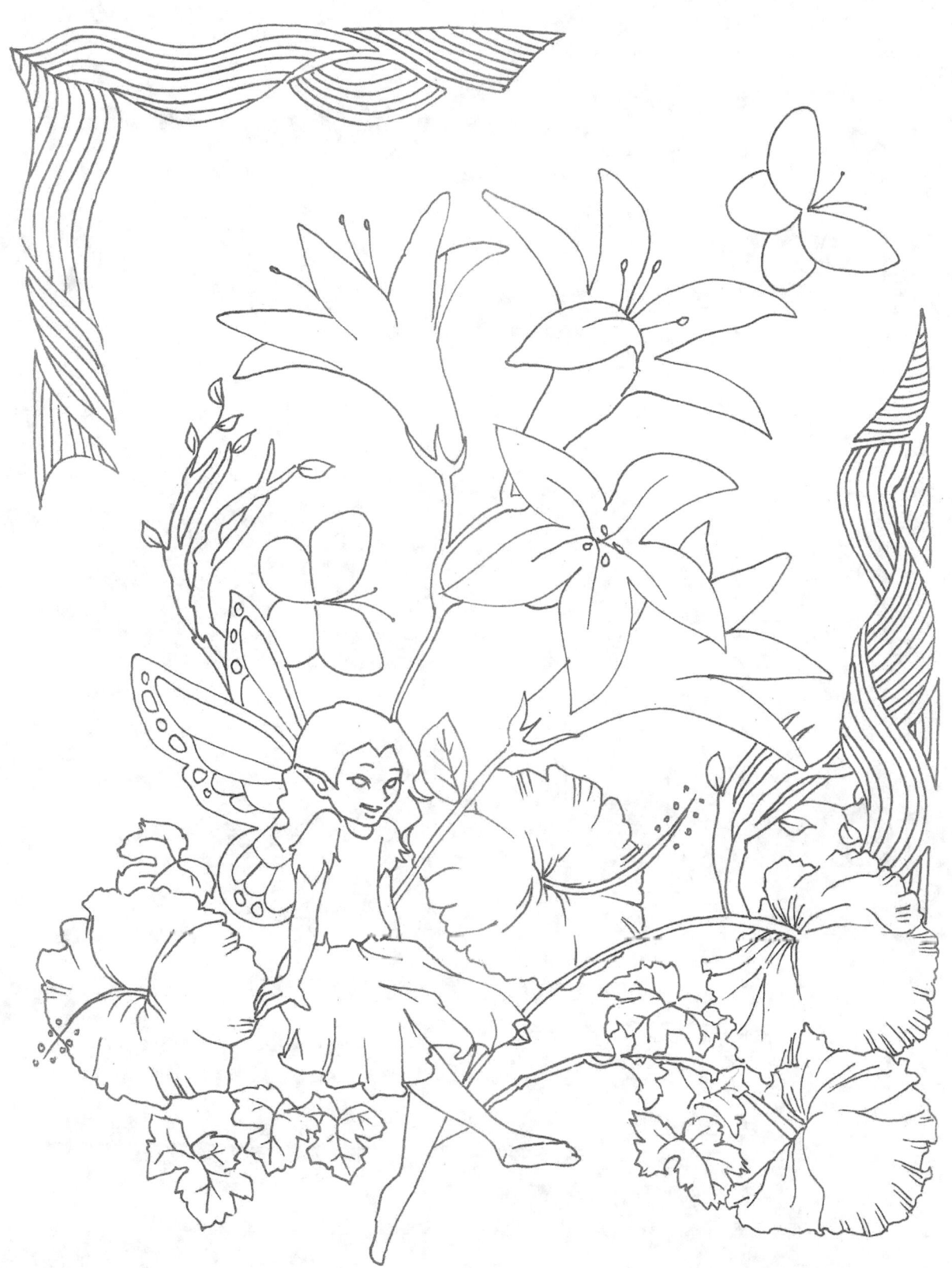

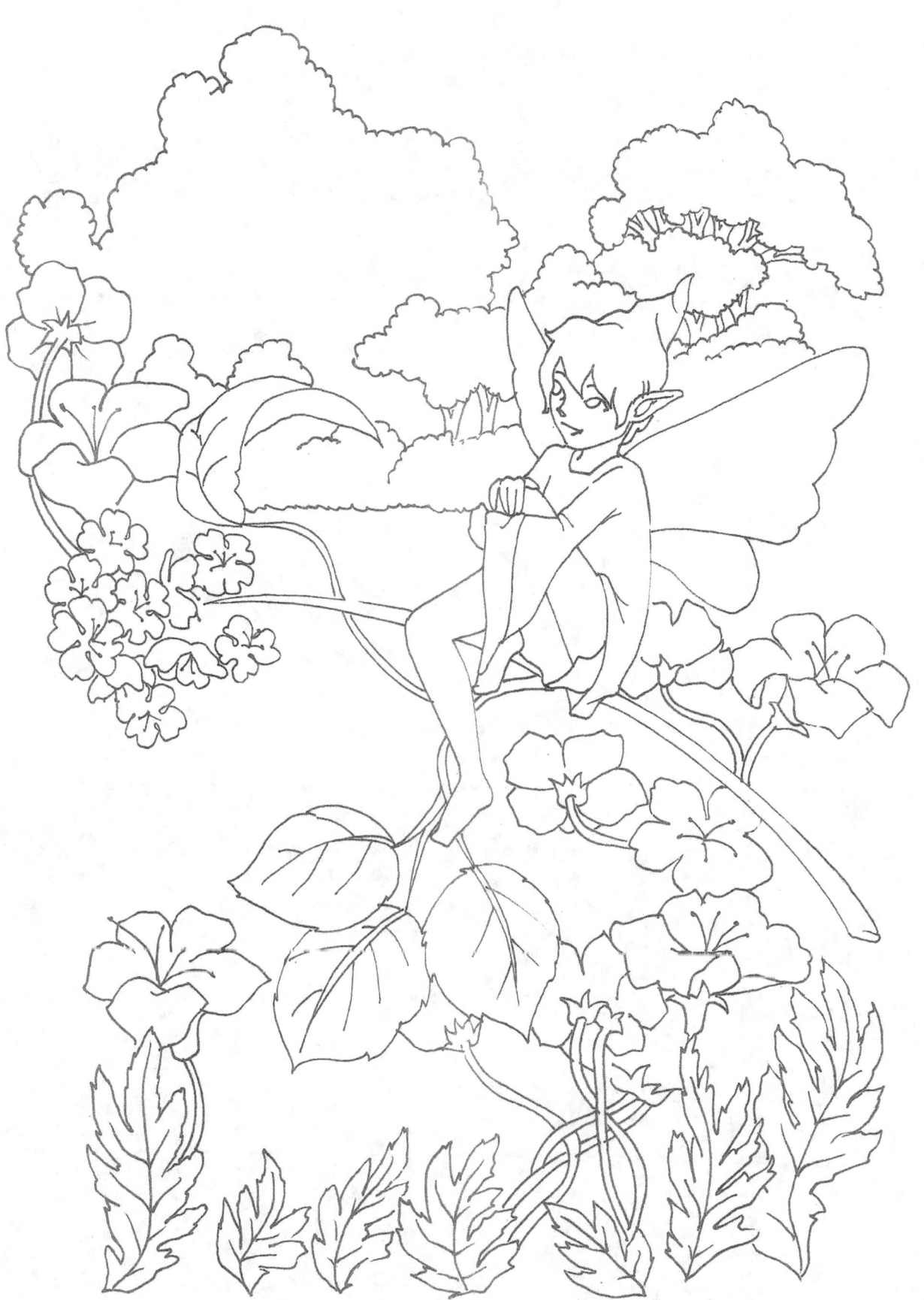

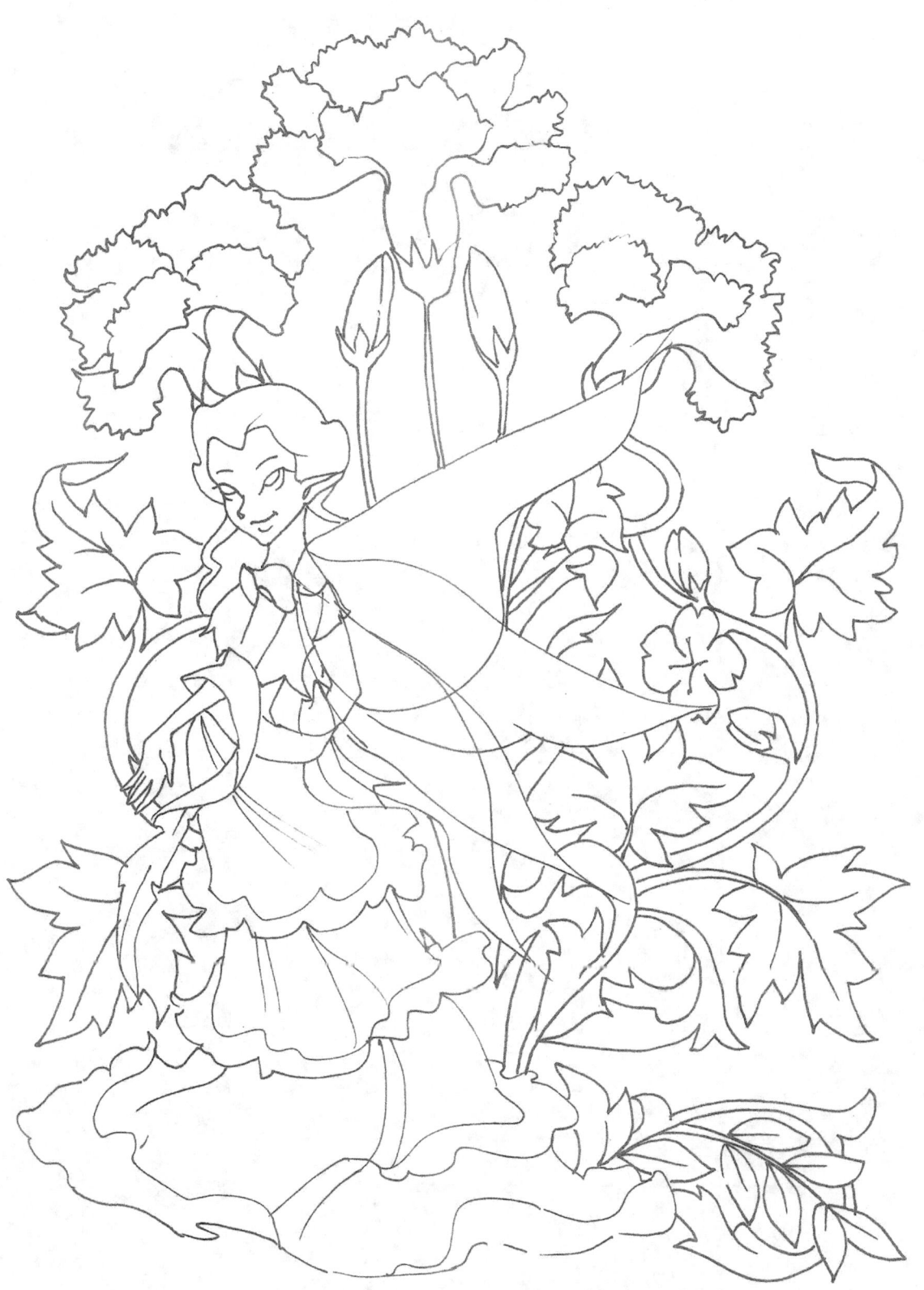

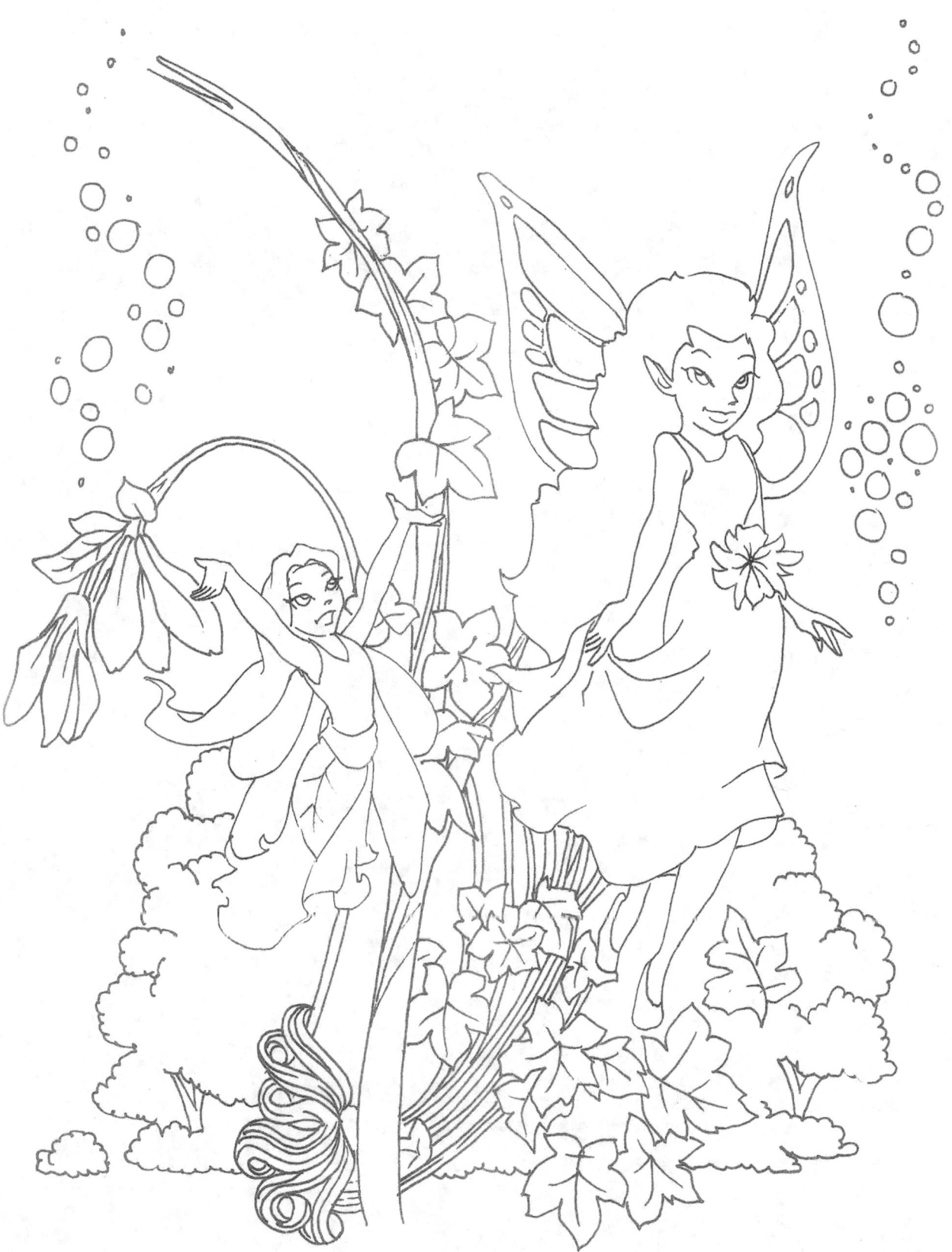

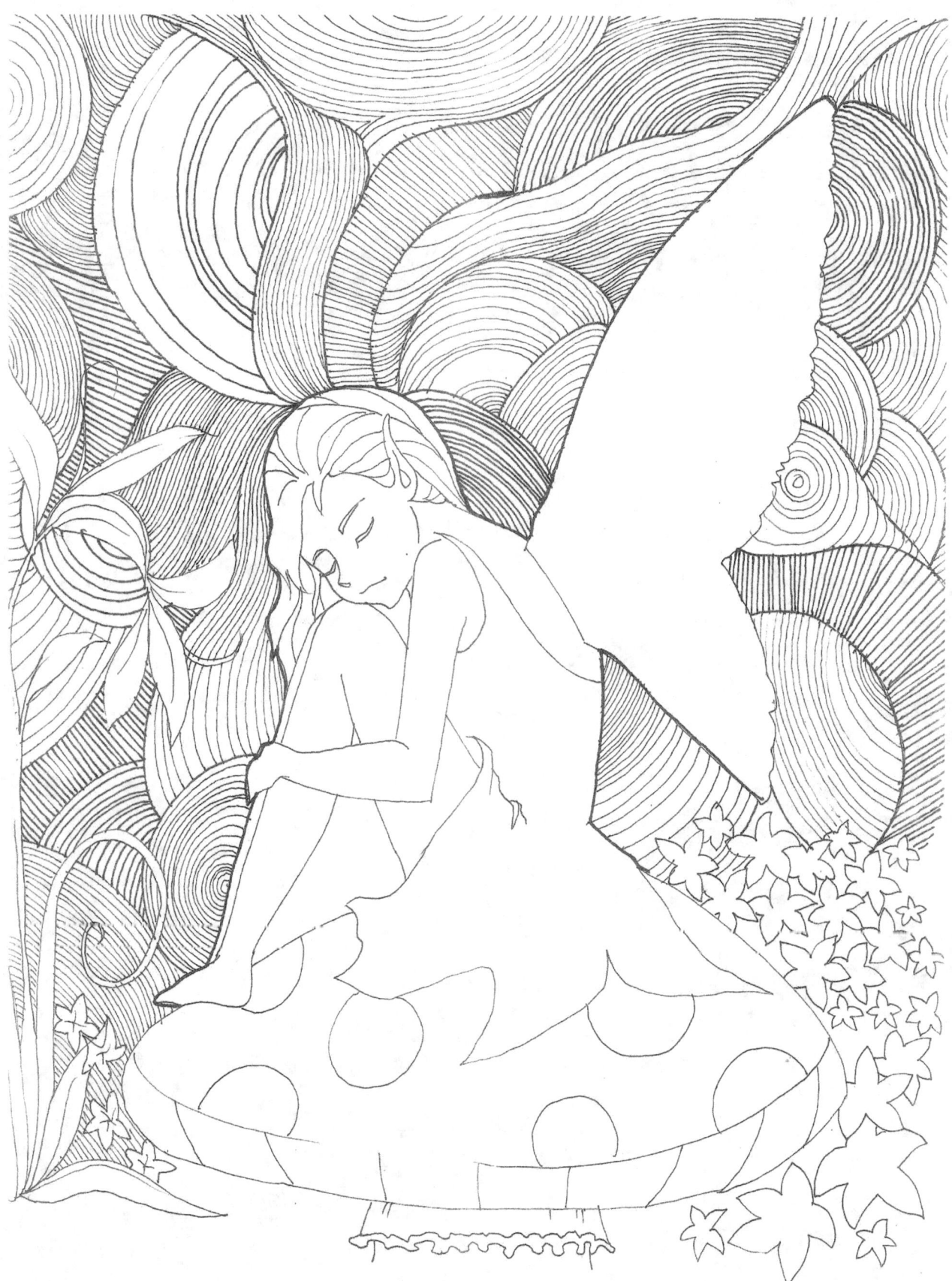

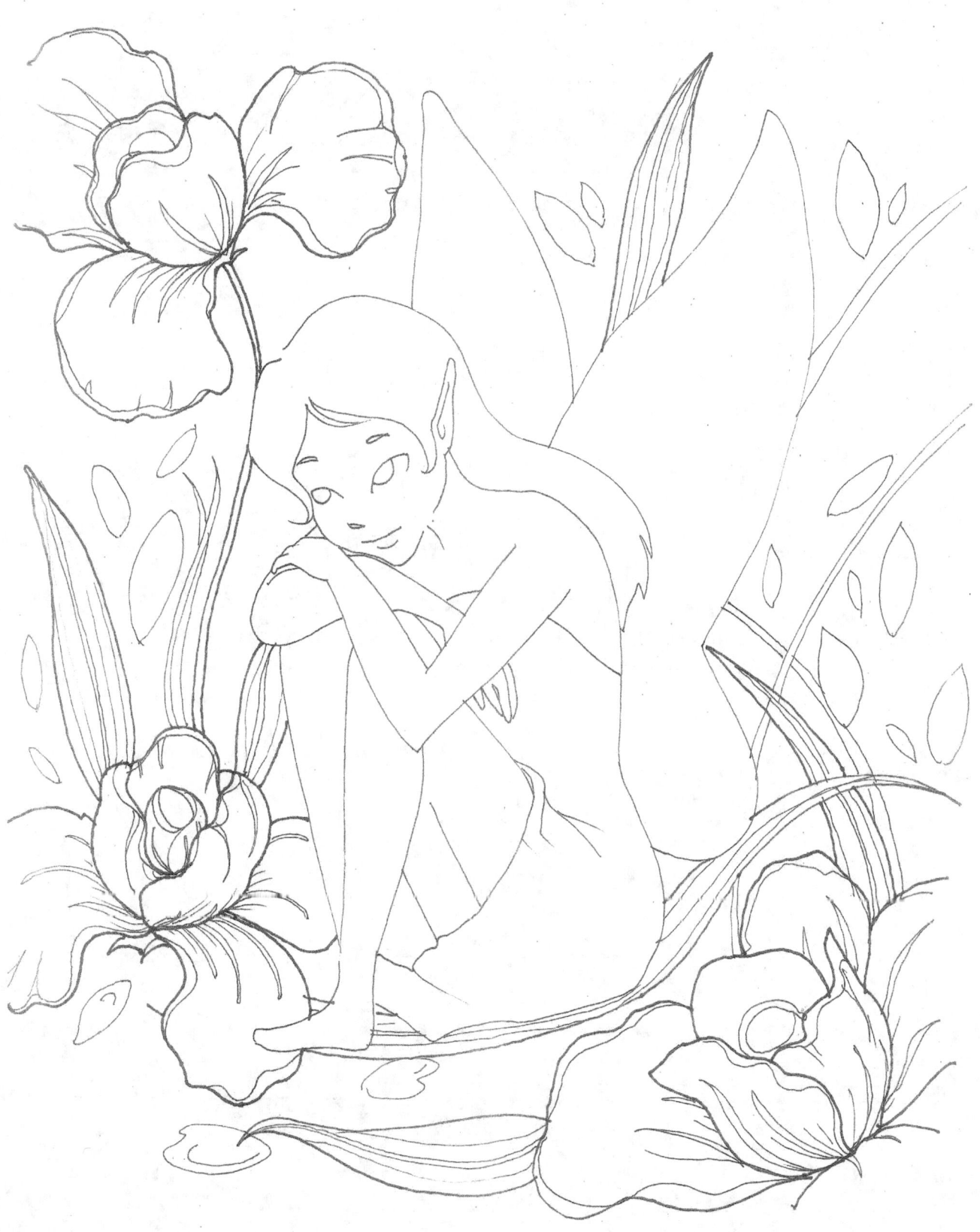

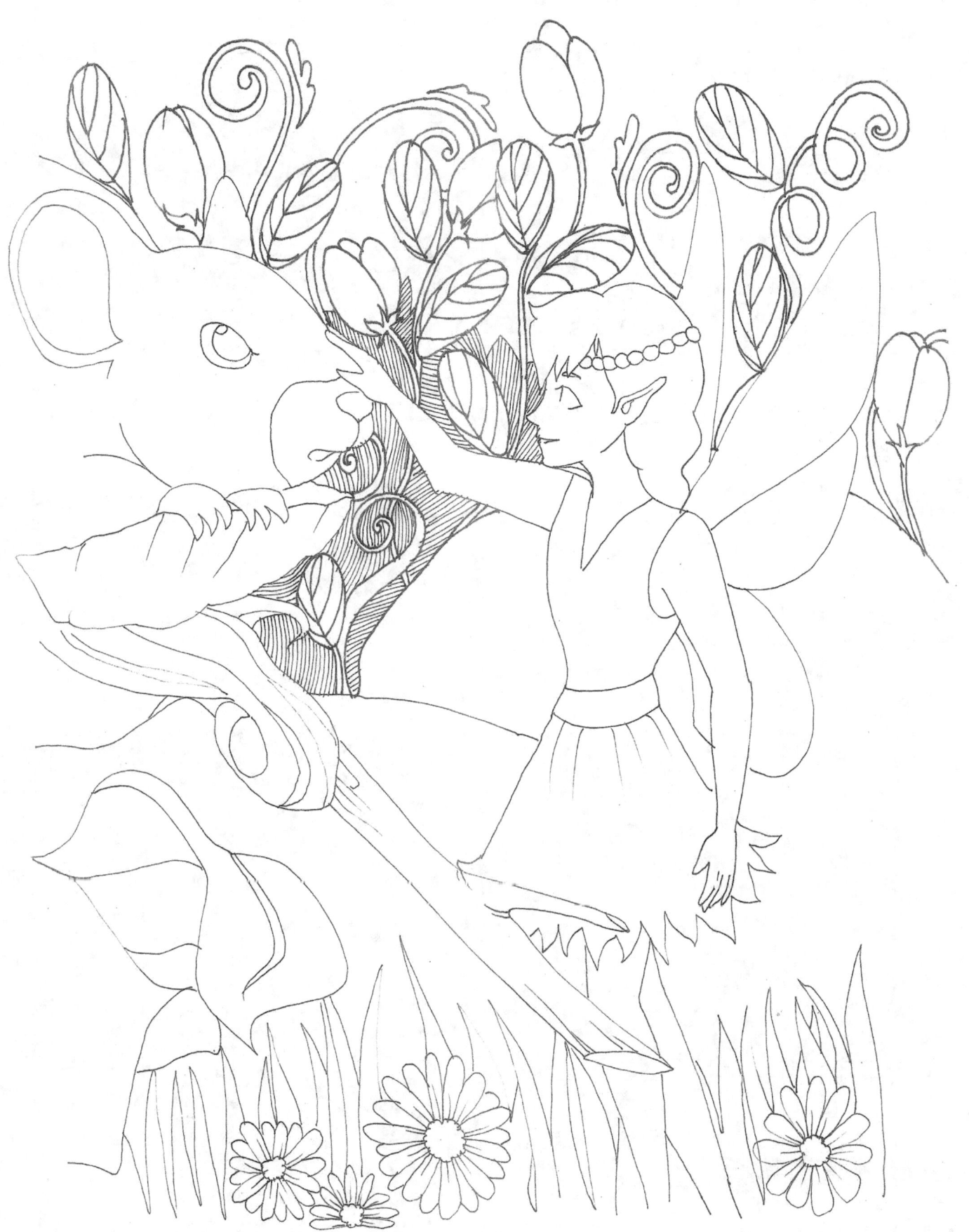

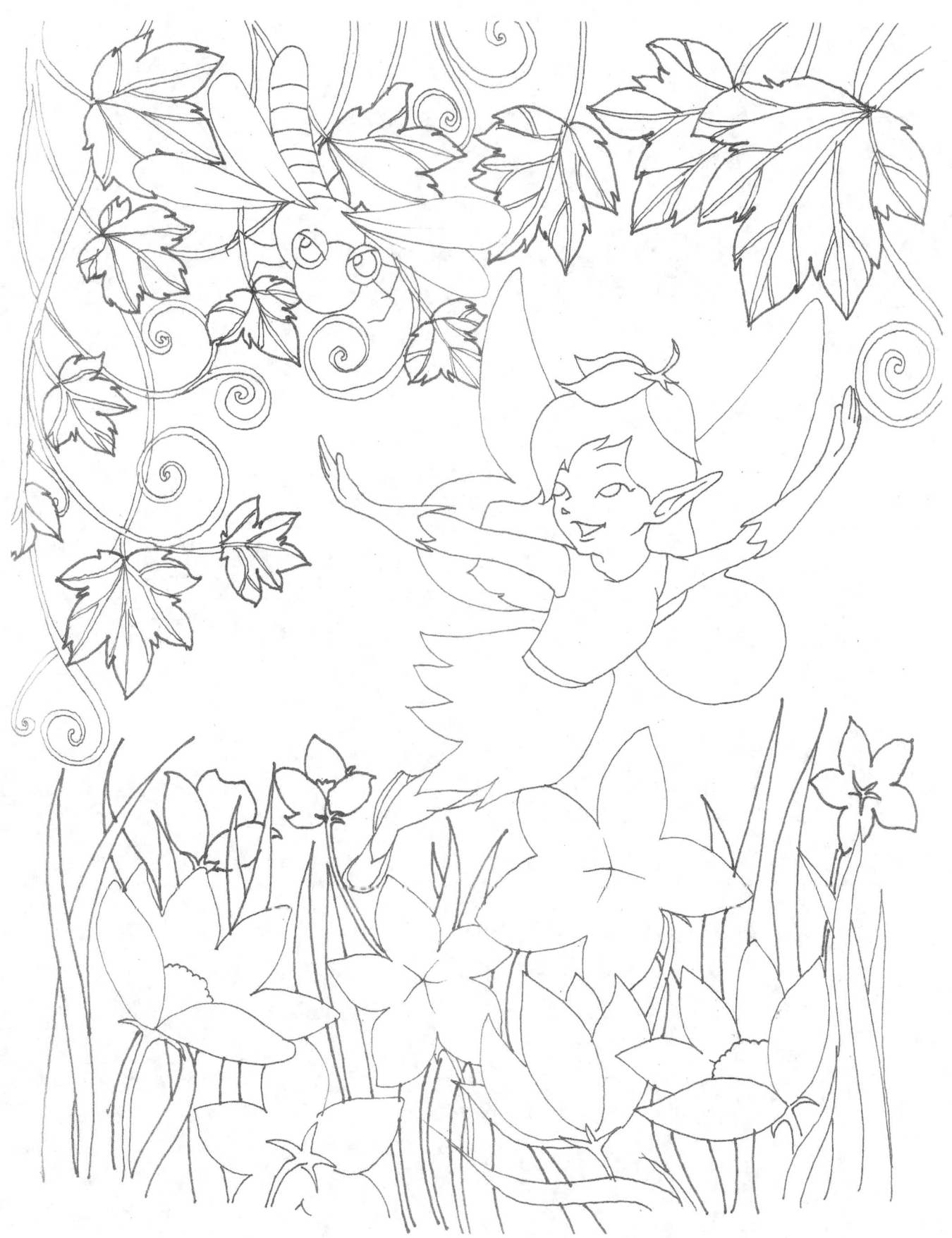

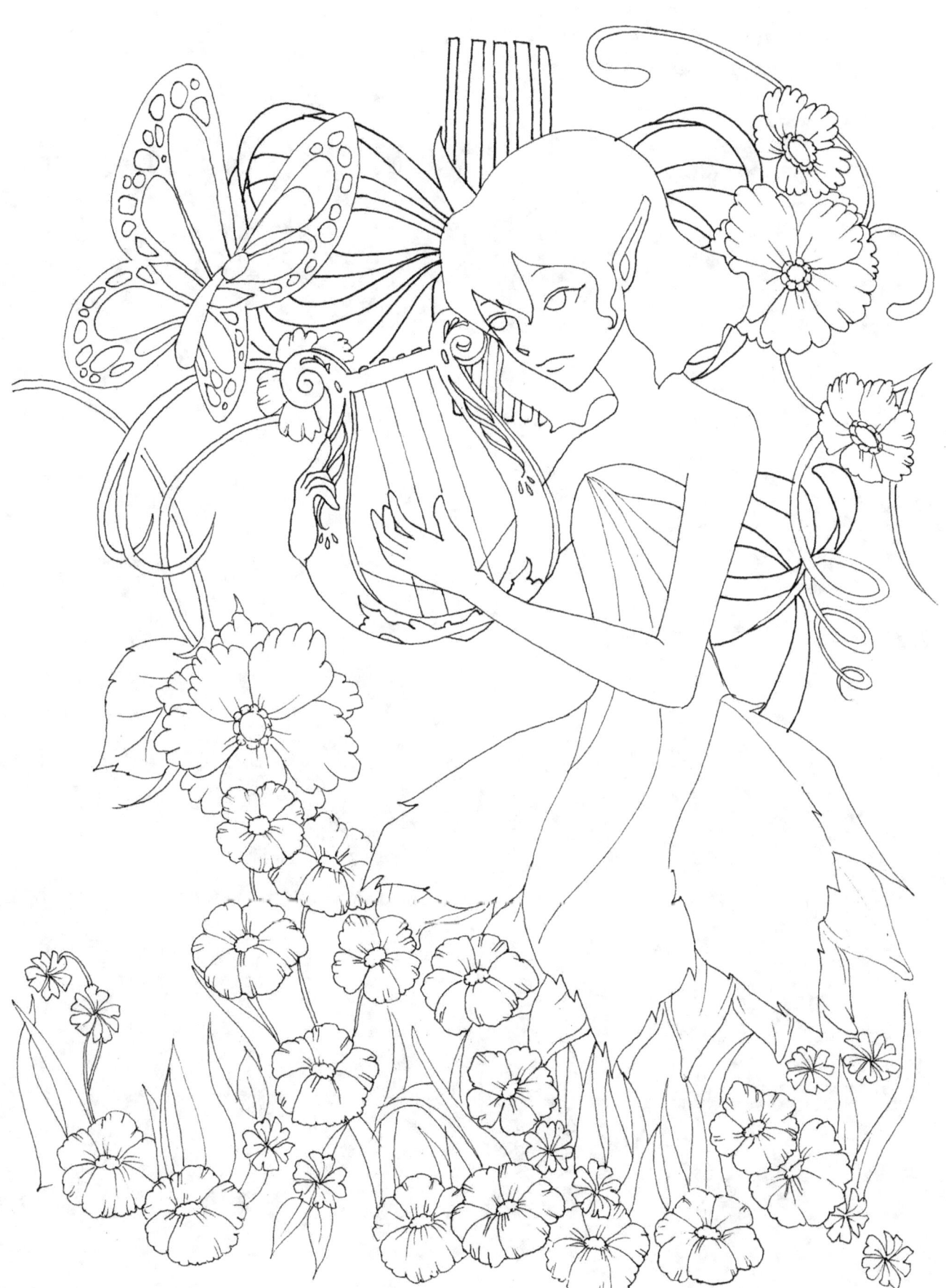

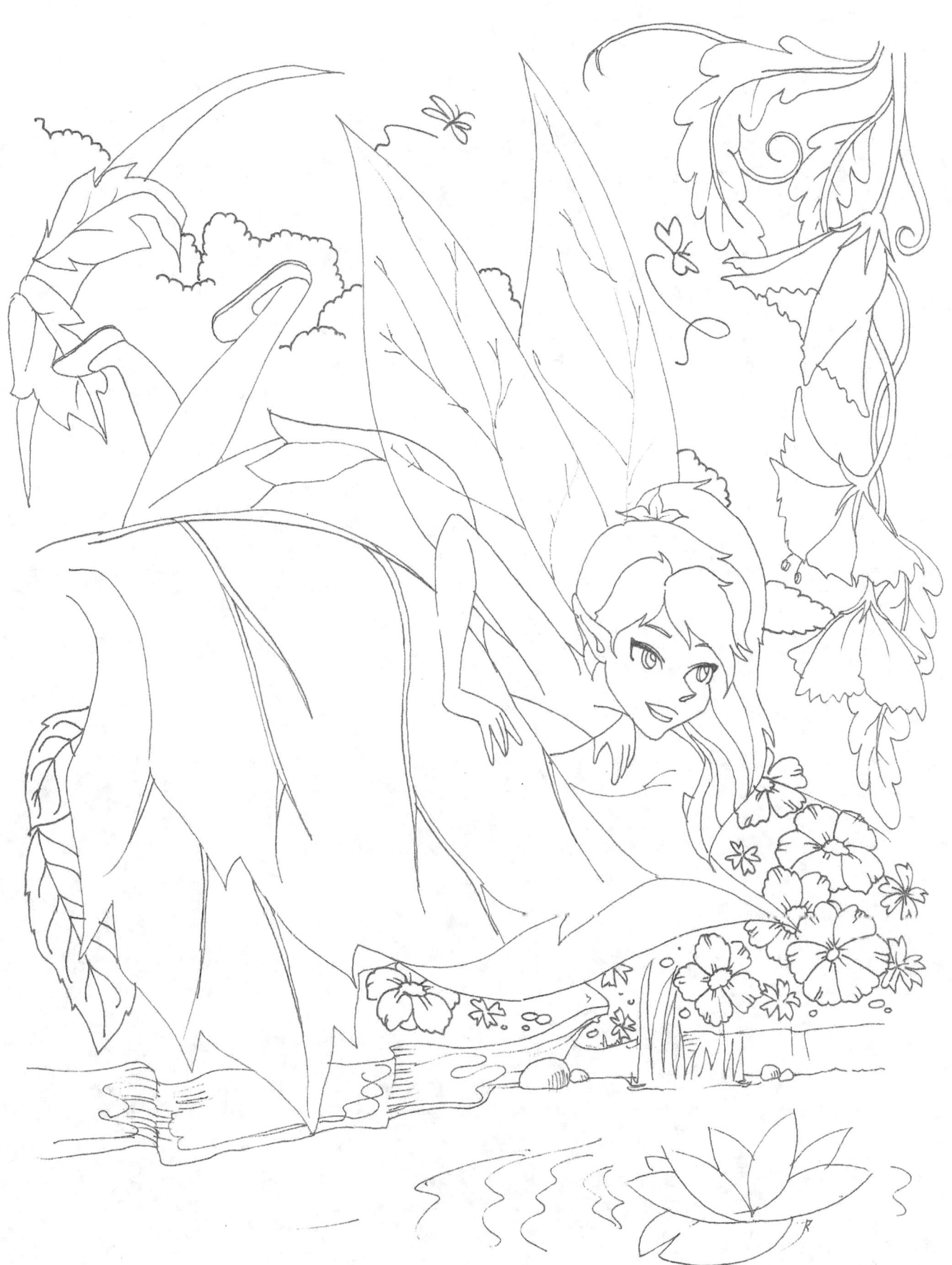

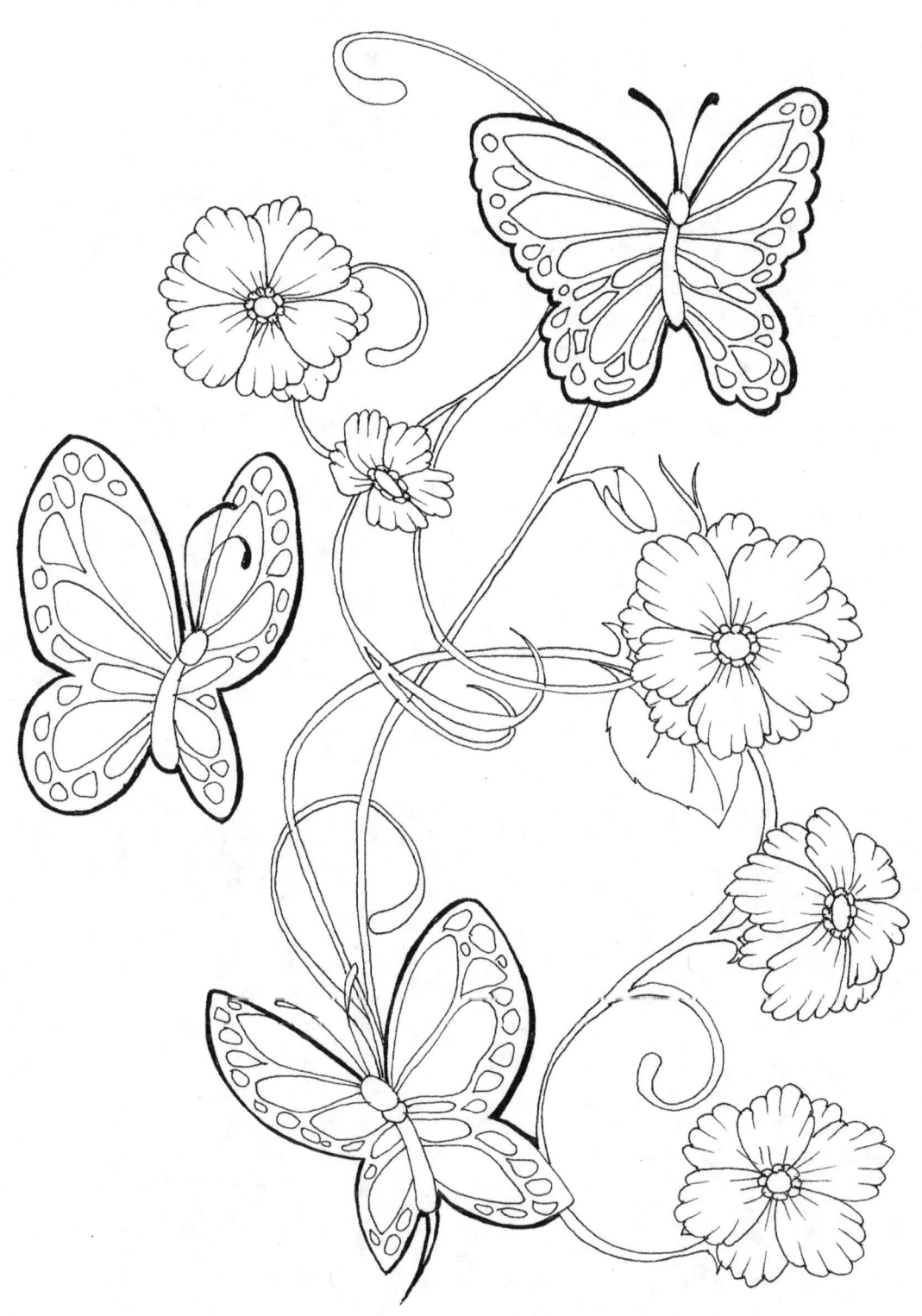

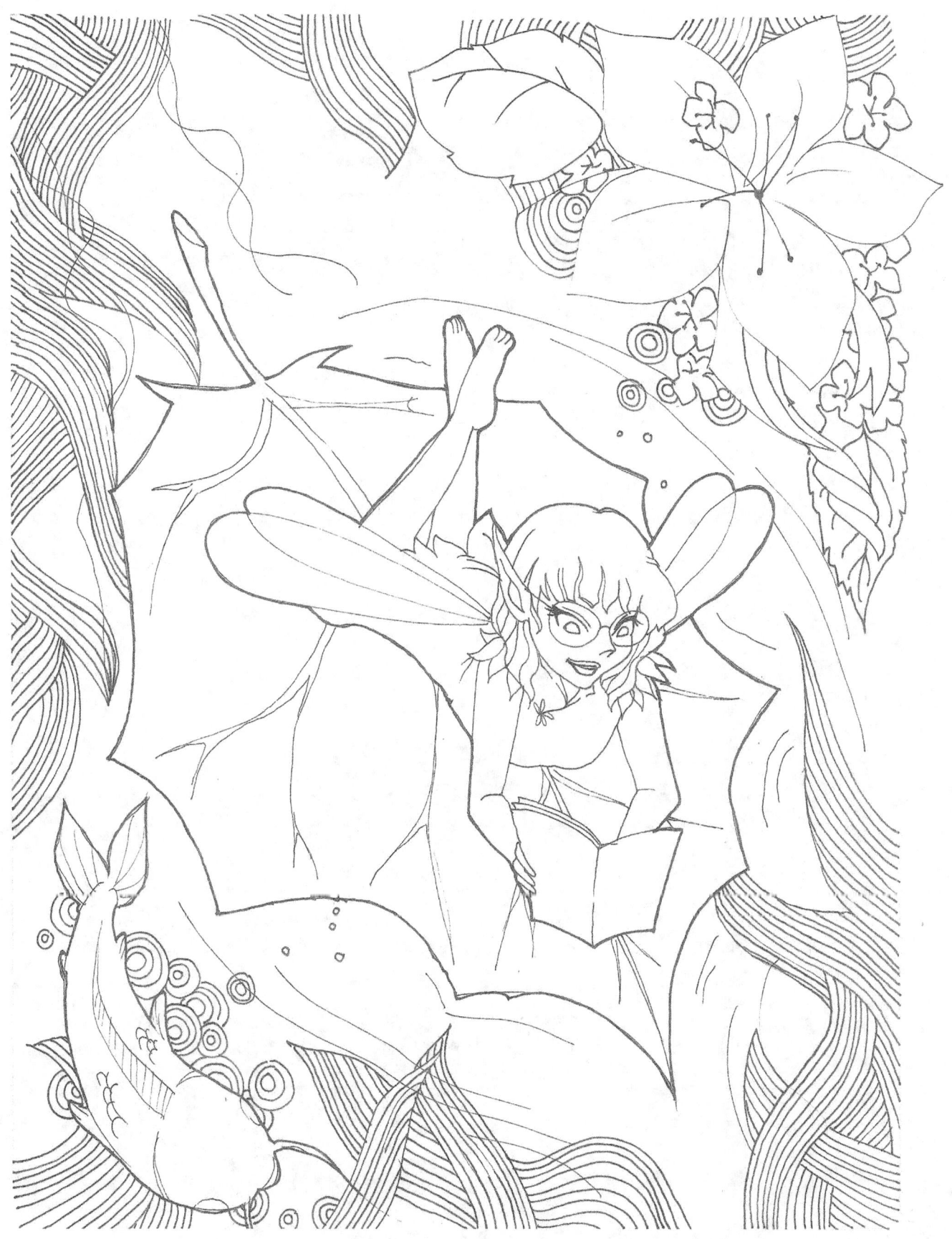

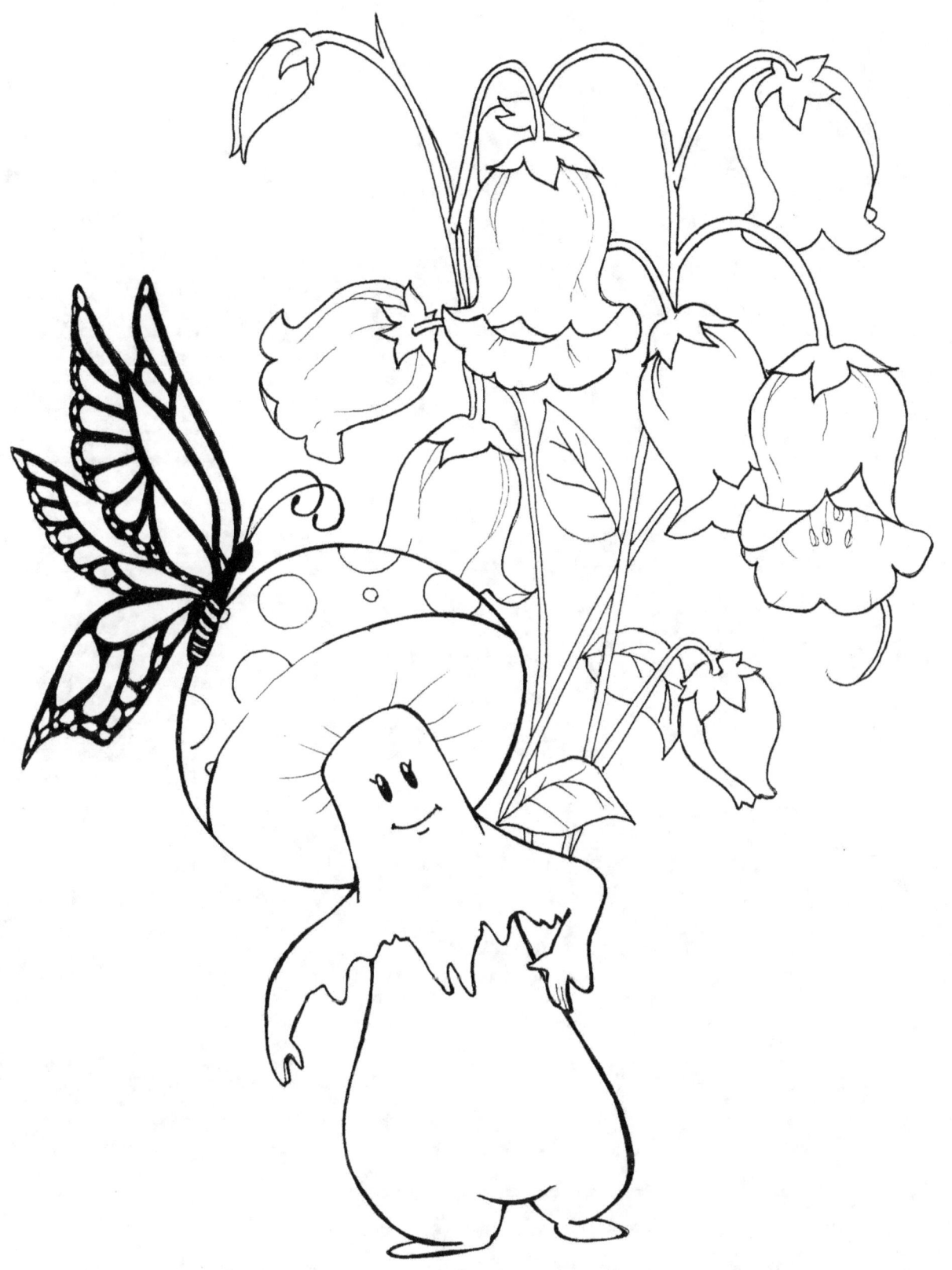

www.ingramcontent.com/pod-product-compliance
Lightning Source LLC
Chambersburg PA
CBHW081743220526
45468CB00008B/2219